示範單位
Show Flat

潘惠森
Poon Wai-sum, Paul

英文翻譯 **潘詩韻**
English Translation Janice Poon, Jai Day

普通話翻譯 **司文、王昊然**
Mandarin Translation Svan, Wang Haoran

香港藝術節委約及製作
Commissioned & produced by
the Hong Kong Arts Festival

Foreword

As with the child, when a play leaves the playwright's hands, many people get involved to guide its progress. A production team puts the work on stage in front of an audience, who then co-create the living experience of theatre in performance. This is the first step in the life of a new play.

Many people are needed again for the next step. The Hong Kong Arts Festival HKAF New Play Selection in book and e-book form, aims to facilitate the journey beyond a HKAF premiere season to subsequent stagings, new productions and new audiences.

I thank my colleagues who continue to inspire me with their dedication. With the team, I thank all the artists and co-creators who make the HKAF a living reality. It is a mark of Hong Kong's sophistication and maturity in theatre making that the new plays presented in the HKAF are warmly anticipated by an audience ready to participate in the co-creation. I look forward to journey towards higher trajectories in the years beyond the 40th HKAF.

Tisa Ho

Executive Director, Hong Kong Arts Festival

前言

劇作跟孩子的成長歷程類同,當一部劇作脫離編劇之手,許多人會參與舞台劇的製作過程,而在現場表演的一刻,觀眾其實也一起共同創作活現在舞台上戲劇的真實體驗。這就是新劇開展生命的第一步。

下一步需要更多人的參與,香港藝術節《新劇本選》的實體書及電子書系列將新劇作品在藝術節首演後推廣到更多舞台、新的製作團隊和新的觀眾群中。

我要感謝我的同事,他們全情投入的熱誠不斷為我帶來新靈感。我和我的團隊要感謝所有參演的藝術家及共同創作者,香港藝術節因有了你們才能如此生動真實。觀眾對香港藝術節呈獻的新劇報以熱切期待,並積極參與,這標誌着香港戲劇已邁向細緻和成熟的階段。我期待香港戲劇在第 40 屆香港藝術節往後的年月中能躍升至更高平台。

何嘉坤
香港藝術節行政總監

Playwright's Notes

The 32nd letter to AA

A. A,

Do you still remember Dumbo? That day when I walked along the tram rail heading west and almost reached Mount Davis, I met him unexpectedly. He passed by like a soulless phantom. I shouted, "Hey! Dumbo!" He was surprised when he recognised me. I asked him, "Where're ya goin'?" "Nowhere. Just wanna find a tree and smoke."

I said you can smoke anywhere without anything; why on earth would you need a tree? With a melancholy voice, he told me his philosophy, "As a city, Hong Kong is one with many trees, but almost all of the trees within urban areas are sick. If I'm lucky, if I find a healthy one, full of life, I'll stop for a while to take a longer look, and light my cigarette under the shade of that tree; it's such a pleasure and bliss, and a healthy thing to do as well, 'cause when you smoke, you also inhale the aura of the tree. When the smoke and the aura mix together in your mouth, they become an organic food."

Maybe you still remember, Dumbo is in fact not an idiot, but just stubborn, while his stubbornness makes him look dull. However, "Duh-brain", as a nickname, is not catchy enough, therefore we decided to call him "Dumbo". I am also a smoker. After receiving his lecture, I could but help tell him with a caring heart, "In our era, smoking has already been stigmatised as a devil's deed; to make your life easier and healthier, it'd be wise to keep your great speech in your mouth with that healthy organic essence." Actually what I was worrying about was that he would be locked away in an asylum. But he replied firmly, "I am a straightforward person, whose words only go in a straight and forward manner; external pressure can change nothing in me."

I decided to end this pointless conversation; there was no point in stopping him if his calling was to be a martyr. So I pointed to the grove along the roadside at the foot of the hill, and said, "Can't you see many trees over

4

編者的話

給 A.A. 的第三十二封信

A.A.：

還記得傻鴻嗎？那天，我在中環沿着電車路西行，快到摩星嶺的時候，不期而遇上他。他像一隻幽靈，飄過我身旁，我大喝一聲：「喂！傻鴻！」他才驚覺我的存在。我問他：「去哪？」他說：「不去哪，只想找棵樹，抽根煙。」我說你抽煙就抽煙，為何要找樹？他語帶幽怨地告訴我這樣一個道理：「香港算是一個多樹的城市，但鬧市的樹十之八九都有病。偶然遇到一棵健康而活潑的，我會停一停，多看兩眼，在樹蔭下抽根煙，那是莫大的享受與幸福，而且十分健康，因為每吸一口，你都順帶把那樹的樹氣吸進去，煙霧和樹氣在口腔混和之後，是一種有機食品。」

也許你還記得，傻鴻其實不傻，只是有點偏執，因偏執而顯得鈍，叫鈍鴻不夠鏗鏘，因此我們才叫他傻鴻。我也是個吸煙的人，聽完傻鴻一番話，禁不住語重心長地告訴他：「現在吸煙已被妖魔化，你這些言論最好不要跟別人說，否則一定惹來炮彈橫飛，死於非命。」我其實真正擔心的是，他會被關進精神病院。他卻堅定地告訴我：「我是一個老實人，老實人只講老實話，外圍壓力不能改變我心中所想。」

我不想跟他囉嗦了，既然他要做烈士，我沒理由反對，便指着路旁山邊一片樹叢，說：「那邊不是有很多樹嗎？趕快去抽你的煙吧，小心不要引起山火。」他有點不屑地告訴我：「我剛從那裏出來，找不到我要找的。」我開始不耐煩了，便說：「做人何必那麼執着呢？你這不就是只見樹木不見林嗎？」他不理我，繼續前行，我隱約聽到他喃喃地說了幾句話。

那天回到家，不知為甚麼，我找出阿城的《樹王》重讀一遍，心頭震撼一如往昔。小說中的「樹王」最終被放倒那一刻，是那麼悲壯，令我感嘆樹的意志終究敵不過人。然後，我又想起傻鴻，

5

there? Go there to take your cigarette. Just be cautious not to burn the woods." He responded with a cold-shouldered arrogance, "It's where I came from; there's nothing I need there." I started to lose my patience, and said, "How come you make your life so rigid? Are you failing to see the wood for the trees?" He ignored me and kept walking forward. It seemed that he was whispering a few words when he left .

That day after I returned home, for no specific reason, I took out Acheng's *Tree King* and read it again. The impact was as strong it had been in the past. It was such a heroic tragedy when, in the novel, the Tree King was eventually taken down, making me sigh at the fact that the will power of the tree cannot overcome those of the human beings at the end. Then I remembered Dumbo, together with his last words, "What I need is just a tree, a healthy tree full of life. What the hell do I need to see the wood for?"

With Dumbo's words lingering in my mind, I finished *Show Flat*. In the Flat, maybe you'll notice the trace of Dumbo. When was the last time you met him? Will you come to watch?

Poon Wai-sum, Paul
15th Dec 2011

Poon Wai-sum, Paul
潘惠森

編劇及導演
Director & Playwright
新域劇團藝術總監
Artistic Director of Prospects Theatre Company

以及他最後那幾句喃喃的自語：「我要的只是一棵樹，一棵健康而活潑的樹，我為甚麼要見林呢？」

在傻鴻縈繞不去的話音中，我完成了《示範單位》。「單位」內，說不定會有傻鴻的身影，你多久沒見過他呢？你會來看嗎？

潘惠森
2011 年 12 月 15 日

《示範單位》首演於第 40 屆香港藝術節，
2012 年 2 月 16 日，香港大會堂劇院
Show Flat premiered at the 40th Hong Kong Arts Festival,
Theatre, Hong Kong City Hall,
16 February 2012.

編劇及導演 Playwright & Director
潘惠森 Poon Wai-sum, Paul

佈景設計 Set Designer
陳友榮 Ewing Chan

服裝及造型設計 Costume & Image Designer
甄紫薇 Annabel Yan

燈光設計 Lighting Designer
劉銘鏗 Lau Ming-hang

音樂及音響設計 Music & Sound Designer
陳偉發 Chan Wai-fat

錄像設計 Video Designer
馮國基 Fung Kwok-kee, Gabriel

製作經理 Production Manager
張向明 Cheung Heung-ming

監製 Producer
香港藝術節 Hong Kong Arts Festival

主演 Cast

Ken

張錦程
Emotion Cheung Kam-ching

阿強
Keung

陳曙曦
Chan Chu-hei

黃金
Goldy

陳淑儀
Chan Suk-yi

辛西蘭
New Seeland

邵美君
Shaw Mei-kwan

歐陸
Eu Look

劉守正
Lau Sau-ching, Bobby

第一場

Scene 1

Scene 1

A show flat.

Keung is in the show flat. He is pretending to talk to someone.

Keung: So?... How do you feel?... Indeed, it's quite good in Hong Kong... I persist when it comes to living. I won't even consider something if it isn't good enough, like you... No, no, no, no, I'm not saying you are a flat. I'm talking about quality... I mean it. You really do look like Shu Qi... No, no, no, no... I mean, you don't just look like her, you are better looking than her... Of course, I chose to spend three years courting you... You can't be compared to those young "models" in Mongkok. I would spend a few days with them, fuck them, and be done... That's not courting, that's just a bit of fun How?... It's like catching butterflies...

Keung starts to catch butterflies.

A door in the show flat opens. Ken enters.

Keung doesn't notice Ken. He continues until the butterflies fly out of the window.

Keung stares after the disappearing butterflies.

Ken coughs and Keung becomes aware of him.

Keung: …

Ken: You are…

Keung: Mr Leung?

Ken: Me?

Keung: When did you arrive?

Ken: Um…

Keung signals Ken to be quiet.

第一場

【一個樓盤的示範單位】

【一個男人在單位內，他是阿強。阿強像在對一個他自己投射出來的「人」說話】

阿強：　So？…How do you feel？…關於住房這件事呢，我真的很執着，沒有一定素質的房子，我真的看不上眼……就好像你這樣……No, no, no, no…我不是說你像一棟房子，我講的是質素，Quality…真的，我真的覺得你長得好像舒淇……No, no, no, no…我是說你貌似舒淇，但是更勝舒淇……當然了，我打算用三年時間追你……當然了，你不是旺角那些嫩模啊，旺角那些嫩模我三天就搞定把她上了……那不是追，是釣……怎樣追？……就好像撲蝶那樣囉……

【阿強撲蝶】

【單位內的一道門打開，一個男人出，他是 Ken】

【阿強沒有注意到 Ken 的出現，繼續撲他的「蝶」，直至他的「蝶」飛出單位】

【阿強目送他的「蝶」消失】

【Ken 發出咳嗽聲】

阿強：　……

Ken：　你是……

阿強：　梁先生？

Ken：　我？

阿強：　什麼時候到的？

Ken：　嗯……

【阿強示意他不要出聲】

Pause.

Keung: Do you hear it?

Ken: What?

Keung: "Click".

Ken: What?

Keung: Men have personalities and so do flats. Men and flats have to "click" with each other. If not, don't take it even if it is free. When you moved just now, "click," I heard it clearly. This flat and you are meant for each other. You have "clicked".

Ken: I think…

Keung: Mr Leung, I am a practical person. You shouldn't look down on these flats. We have jargon for this kind of flat, "quick sellers". They are high quality, that's why they sell quickly. Delay no more. This is a show flat, the last one. Buy now! Live now!

Ken signals Keung to hold on.
Ken answers his mobile.

Ken: Hello, Mr Ng… Yes, I am here… no problem… take your time… it looks fine… Of course, men have personalities and so do flats. Men and flats have to "click" with each other. If not, don't take it even if it is free, right?... Sure… no problem… take your time… I will wait for you.

Ken hangs up.

Keung: You mother fucker…

Ken: You were saying…

Keung: Men have personality, and so do flats.

Ken: I like wise quotes.

Keung: I should charge you royalties.

【靜默片刻】

阿強： 聽到沒有？

Ken： 吓？

阿強： 啪一聲。

Ken： 什麼啪一聲啊？

阿強： 人有人格，屋有屋格。人格和屋格一定要合，不合的話送給你都不能要，你剛才身子一動，啪一聲，我聽得很清楚，這間房子跟你，合拍，杠杠的！

Ken： 我想你……

阿強： 梁先生，我做事真的很實在，這批貨真的不簡單，在我們行內有個名號，叫做「詠春」貨，為什麼叫「詠春」貨呢？因為它質量好，賣得快，咻咻咻，一猶豫你就中招，這套房是示範單位，最後一個，即買即住。Buy now！Live now！

【Ken 示意阿強等一等】

【Ken 接聽手機】

Ken： 喂，吳先生……是啊，我到了……沒問題……慢慢來，不要急……看起來都 OK 的……當然啦，正所謂「人有人格，屋有屋格，人格和屋格一定要合，不合的話送給你都不能要」，對不對？……當然啦……沒問題……不用急……我等你。

【Ken 收起電話】

阿強： 媽了個逼的……

Ken： 你剛才說到……

阿強： 人有人格，屋有屋格。

Ken： 我很喜歡這種智慧名言。

阿強： 我是不是應該先跟你收版權費啊？

Ken: Royalties?

Keung: We are in the same industry. You just put your hands in my pockets…

Ken: OK.

Ken takes out his purse.

Ken: I will pay for it.

Keung: …

Ken takes out a bank note and hands it to Keung.

Ken: A thousand.

Keung: …

Ken: Too little?

Keung tries to take the note. Ken moves away suddenly.

Ken: Is the world round?

Keung: What?

Ken: Answer me.

Keung: Fuck you…

Ken: Is the world round?

Keung: Yes.

Ken: Again?

Keung: The world is round.

Ken: Columbus said this. Do you pay him royalties?

Keung: …

Ken puts the note back in his wallet.

Ken: If you don't have to pay him, why should I pay you? Keung.

Ken：	版權？
阿強：	大家都是吃這碗飯，你現在現偷現賣拿我的……
Ken：	OK.
	【Ken 拿出錢包】
Ken：	我給。
阿強：	……
	【Ken 取出一張鈔票遞給阿強】
Ken：	一千。
阿強：	……
Ken：	嫌太少？
	【阿強伸手接鈔票，Ken 忽然把鈔票拿開】
Ken：	地球是不是圓的？
阿強：	什麼意思？
Ken：	先回答我。
阿強：	Fuck you.
Ken：	地球是不是圓的？
阿強：	Yes!
Ken：	講清楚一點？
阿強：	地球是圓的。
Ken：	這句話是哥倫布說的，你是不是要付他版權費啊？
阿強：	……
	【Ken 收回鈔票】
Ken：	如果你不用給他的話，為什麼我要給你呢？阿強。

Keung:	…
Ken:	Veggie Keung.
Keung:	…
Ken:	Do you recognise me?
Keung:	…
Ken:	I am Ken.
Keung:	…
Ken:	Baldly Ken.
Keung:	You mother fucker…
Ken:	You still like to swear!
Keung:	You've turned hairy?
Ken:	Hair grows…
Keung:	Isn't it a wig?
Ken:	It's real. Touch it…
	Keung touches Ken's hair.
Keung:	It's real…
Ken:	Of course…
	Keung pulls Ken's hair suddenly.
Ken:	Ouch!
Keung:	You fucking ass hole…
Ken:	Hey, wait, wait…
Keung:	This is real…
Ken:	Let go of me!
	Ken pushes Keung away.

阿強： ……

Ken： 蔡遠強。

阿強： ……

Ken： 你真的認不出我來？

阿強： ……

Ken： 阿 Ken 啊。

阿強： ……

Ken： 禿頭 Ken 啊！

阿強： 媽了個逼的……

Ken： 還這麼喜歡說髒話！

阿強： 你現在頭髮真雞巴多啊。

Ken： 長回來了嘛……

阿強： 假髮來的吧……

Ken： 真的，你摸一下……

【阿強摸 Ken 的頭髮】

阿強： 還真是喔……

Ken： 當然啦……

【阿強忽然扯 Ken 的頭髮】

Ken： 哎啊！

阿強： 操你媽的……

Ken： 喂喂喂！

阿強： 果然是真的喔……

Ken： 放手！

【Ken 推開阿強】

19

Keung:	Ken!
Ken:	Don't get any closer.
Keung:	You are Baldly Ken!
Ken:	Get away from me…
Keung:	Haven't seen you for three decades…
Ken:	You keep pulling…
Keung :	You got so hairy?
Ken:	It won't grow again, you bastard!
Keung :	*(Sings) This time, this place, this face…*
Ken:	Didn't you join the gangs?
Keung :	Who said that?
Ken:	Cocky.
Keung :	Fatty Cocky?
Ken	Yes.
Keung :	He's still alive?
Ken:	The last time I saw him was in 97…
Keung :	Many people have died since 97, he must be one of them.
Ken:	Many people died but why the hell are you still alive?
Keung :	Good point.
Ken:	It's a joke.
Keung :	How do you know this person in front of you is not a ghost?
Ken:	Are you trying to frighten me?
Keung :	The more ghosts compete, the less we get. Fuck you.
Ken:	…

阿強： 阿 Ken！

Ken： 你別過來……

阿強： 原來你真是禿頭 Ken！

Ken： 離我遠點……

阿強： 20 多年沒見……

Ken： 不能再扯了……

阿強： 竟然頭髮都長回來了？！

Ken： 再掉就長不回來了，媽的！

阿強： （唱）此時，此地，此模樣……

Ken： 你不是去當古惑仔了嗎？

阿強： 誰跟你說的？

Ken： 阿雞。

阿強： 肥雞？

Ken： 是啊。

阿強： 他還沒死嗎？

Ken： 最後一次見他，都已經是 97 年的事啦……

阿強： 97 之後香港死了一屁眼子人，他肯定是其中一個。

Ken： 這麼多人死都不見你死？

阿強： Good point.

Ken： 開玩笑啦。

阿強： 你怎麼知道你現在見到的，不是一隻鬼呢？

Ken： 嚇我啊？

阿強： 多隻香爐多隻鬼啊，Fuck you！

Ken： ……

Keung :	How long have you been in this business?
Ken:	…
Keung :	Less than a year?
Ken:	…
Keung :	It's not too late if you quit now.
Ken:	…
Keung :	Corpses everywhere.
Ken:	How did you know?
Keung :	Corpses everywhere?
Ken	How did you know I was in less than a year?
Keung :	You mother fucker, I can smell it.
Ken	Why don't you join the police?
Keung :	What?
Ken:	Be a police dog.
	Pause.
Ken:	It's a joke.
Keung :	It's fucking funny, you fucking asshole.
Ken:	Can't you take a joke?
	Keung barks at Ken suddenly. Ken is shocked.
Keung :	This is more fun.
	Not wanting to be outdone Ken barks loudly at Keung.
	They bark at each other, like two teenagers in a school playground.
	A sudden, loud noise interrupts them, the sound of a pile driver that seems to freeze time.

阿強： 　啥時候入行的？

Ken： 　……

阿強： 　不到一年。

Ken： 　……

阿強： 　現在撤還來得及。

Ken： 　……

阿強： 　屍橫遍野啊。

Ken： 　你怎麼知道的？

阿強： 　屍橫遍野？

Ken： 　你怎麼知道我入行不到一年啊？

阿強： 　我操你媽的聞都聞得出來啦。

Ken： 　你怎麼不加入警隊啊？

阿強： 　啥意思？

Ken： 　做警犬啊。

　　　　【靜默片刻】

Ken： 　開玩笑啦。

阿強： 　真他媽好笑啊！我日你個小菊花。

Ken： 　連玩笑都不能開一下？

　　　　【阿強忽然扮狗向 Ken 吼了一聲。Ken 被嚇了一跳】

阿強： 　這樣不是更好笑。

　　　　【Ken 不甘示弱，亦扮狗向阿強大吼一聲】

　　　　【兩人一來一往扮狗互相鬥吼／嚇，彷彿回到學生時代】

　　　　【忽然一下巨響 — 是一下打樁聲 — 彷彿把時間凝固了】

第二場

Scene 2

Scene 2

Immediately following the previous scene.

Time moves slowly. As if on a conveyor belt Keung and Ken exit as Eu Look and New Seeland enter.

Eu Look and New Seeland are in their twenties.

The pile driving noise continues.

Look: Here we are.

Seeland: It's noisy here.

          Eu Look takes out two pairs of earplugs, and gives one to New Seeland.

Look: Take them.

Seeland: What are these?

Look: Earplugs.

Seeland: What?

Look: Put them in.

          They put in the earplugs. The pile driving noise is lowered to a background sound.

Seeland: I have to work. Why did you bring me here?

Look: The last one.

Seeland: What?

Look: The last one at this site. The last pile being driven into the ground.

Seeland: I am leaving.

          New Seeland is about to leave. Eu Look stops her.

Look: Listen to me.

第二場

【緊接上場】

【時間慢慢地移動，像一條輸送帶，把阿強和 Ken 帶走的同時，也帶來了歐陸和辛西蘭】

【此時的歐陸和辛西蘭約 20 餘歲】

【打樁聲持續】

歐陸： 到啦，就是這裏。

辛西蘭： 好吵啊。

【歐陸拿出兩對耳塞，一對給辛西蘭】

歐陸： 拿去。

辛西蘭： 什麼來的？

歐陸： 耳塞。

辛西蘭： 吓？

歐陸： 戴上它。

【兩人戴上耳塞，打樁聲馬上降低，成為一種背景聲音】

辛西蘭： 我還要工作啊，你帶我來這兒幹嘛啊？

歐陸： 是最後一條。

辛西蘭： 什麼最後一條啊？

歐陸： 這個地盤最後一條，樁。

辛西蘭： 我先走啦。

【辛西蘭欲下，歐陸把她拉着】

歐陸： 你先聽我講完嘛。

Seeland:	One minute.
Look:	This minute, might be the most crucial 60 seconds in your life.
Seeland:	Tell me.
Look:	A building will grow here very soon.
Seeland:	What does that have to do with you?
Look:	I am excited.
Seeland:	Are you building it?
Look:	Even if I'm not, I am excited
Seeland:	Fifty seconds.
Look:	Listen…
Seeland:	Forty nine.
Look:	Every bang makes my heart beat. Can't you feel it?
Seeland:	My whole body is beating.
Look:	This is pure excitement.
Seeland:	What?
Look:	Don't you feel high now?
Seeland:	…
Look:	Listen with your body.
Seeland:	…
Look:	Close your eyes. Relax… feel it…
Seeland:	I feel like it's transmitting from the ground; from my feet to my heart…
Look:	You feel it?
Seeland:	It's getting stronger…

辛西蘭： 一分鐘。

歐陸： 這一分鐘，可能是你一生中最關鍵的 60 秒。

辛西蘭： 講吧。

歐陸： 很快，這裏就會有一棟房子長出來。

辛西蘭： 關你什麼事呢？

歐陸： 興奮。

辛西蘭： 是你的嗎？

歐陸： 不是也一樣興奮。

辛西蘭： 50 秒。

歐陸： 你聽……

辛西蘭： 49。

歐陸： 每嘭一下，心就會震一下，你不覺得嗎？

辛西蘭： 簡直就是整個人彈起來了好不好……

歐陸： 這就叫做興奮。

辛西蘭： 吓？

歐陸： 你現在是不是有點 High 了？

辛西蘭： ……

歐陸： 你試試用你的身體去聽。

辛西蘭： ……

歐陸： 閉上眼，放輕鬆……感受一下……

辛西蘭： 好像從地下滲上來，從腳底傳到心臟……

歐陸： 你真的有 Feel 到？

辛西蘭： 愈來愈澎湃……

Look:	I know you can.
Seeland:	It's like listening to Beethoven…
Look:	Really?
Seeland:	The frequency is getting higher.
Look:	Stop!
Seeland:	What's wrong with you?
Look:	You have to control it. Stay your imagination. Just keep yourself high, don't go any further. If you do, you will lose control. It has nothing to do with Beethoven.

Pause.

Seeland:	This thing?
Look:	Our relationship.
Seeland:	What's wrong with it?
Look:	Is like this construction site.
Seeland:	Corpses everywhere?
Look:	It's filled with piles, it has a solid foundation.
Seeland:	…
Look:	Today, in front of this site, I promise you, when the last pile is laid, on this solid foundation, our lives will be built with a new look, open up new space, and be full of possibilities.

Pause.

Seeland:	What are you trying to say?
Look:	Marry me.

歐陸：　　我就知道你行。

辛西蘭：　好像是在聽貝多芬……

歐陸：　　沒那麼誇張吧？

辛西蘭：　因為分貝愈來愈高……

歐陸：　　Stop！

辛西蘭：　幹嘛啊？

歐陸：　　你要懂得控制才行，Keep 住你的想像力，Feel 到 High 就好了，不要再往上去，再去你就失控啦，這件事跟貝多芬完全沒關係。

【靜默片刻】

辛西蘭：　這件事？

歐陸：　　我們的感情。

辛西蘭：　什麼事啊？

歐陸：　　就像這個地盤一樣。

辛西蘭：　滿目瘡痍？

歐陸：　　已經打滿了樁，有了一個堅實的基礎。

辛西蘭：　……

歐陸：　　今天，就在這個地盤面前，我向你保証，當最後這支樁打進去，我和你的生命，就會在一個堅實的基礎上面，建構出一個全新的局面，開拓出一個全新的空間，充滿無限的可能。

【靜默片刻】

辛西蘭：　你到底想說什麼啊？

歐陸：　　嫁給我。

New Seeland takes out her ear plugs.

A loud pile driving noise freezes time again.

The frozen time is broken by the noise of dogs barking.

Seeland: What kind of dogs are these ?!

Look: Wolf-dogs.

Both exit.

【辛西蘭從耳朵取出耳塞】

【一下巨大的打樁聲，彷彿又把時間凝固起來】

【這凝固的狀態很快便被一陣狗吠聲打破】

辛西蘭： 嘩，什麼狗來的，叫得這麼兇？！

歐陸： 是兇狗。

【兩人下】

第三場
Scene 3

Scene 3

Immediately after the previous scene.

Time reverses. While New Seeland and Eu Look are towards the exit, Keung and Ken enter. They continue to bark at each other like teenagers.

A door in the show flat opens. A man enters. He is Goldy.

A phone rings.

Goldy takes out a mobile phone, a glittering one.

Goldy: Hello…

The mobile phone lights up the show flat with a beam of golden light.

Goldy continues with his phone conversation.

Goldy: Investing in real estate is like investing in happiness. You don't have it now but you will have it one day. If you have never heard that, I am telling you now…

V.O.: Go tell the mother fucker this is the last one, the last one. If you can't make this deal, you won't have to make shit ever again…

Goldy hangs up.

Goldy: Obviously, we have three ghosts here.

Keung/Ken: …

Goldy: Three ghosts, but only one can survive.

Keung/Ken: …

Goldy: My client will be here soon. If you haven't seen people making deals and you want to learn from me you are more than welcome to stay. Like an internship. I am fine with that. But if you don't want to waste your time *(takes out two coupons)*… Here are two coupons. They will save you two

第三場

【緊接上場】

【時間逆轉－在辛西蘭與歐陸下場的同時，阿強和 Ken 上，仍然保持着第一場結束時的少年狀態，繼續扮狗互相鬥吼 / 嚇】

【單位的一道門打開，走出一個男人 ─ 黃金】

【電話聲】

【黃金拿出電話，是一部金光閃爍的手提電話】

黃金：　喂……

【他的電話恍似一道流金，慢慢把單位染成金黃色】

【黃金繼續講他的電話】

黃金：　投資物業，就是投資幸福。你現在沒有，但將來會有，如果沒人告訴你，我現在告訴你……

V.O.：　講你媽逼啊，最後啦，最後一個啦，搞不定這個你以後就別他媽混了我操！

【黃金收起電話】

黃金：　很明顯，這裏有三隻香爐。

阿強 /Ken：……

黃金：　三隻，只能活一隻。

阿強 /Ken：……

黃金：　我的客戶馬上就到，如果你們沒見過人買房子簽約想學習一下，我非常歡迎，當是 Internship，我無所謂，但是如果你們不想浪費時間 ─（拿出兩張 Coupon）這裏有兩張 Coupon，大快活下午茶可以優惠兩塊錢，我就忍痛割愛了。

dollars on a tea set at Fairwood. Reluctant though I am, you may take them.

Keung/Ken: …

Goldy: Two dollar coupons have monetary value! It took me ages to save up enough points at PARKnSHOP to earn these. If you tear them off, you can see blood and…

Goldy tears off the coupons unconsciously.

Keung/Ken: …

Goldy: (*Licks and sticks the coupons back together*) It can still be used… Cutting Keung, take it and we are even.

Ken: Cutting Keung?

Goldy: Just once…

Ken: When did you start cutting line?

Goldy: Take your partner with you, now.

Keung: He is not my partner.

Ken: I was his schoolmate.

Keung: His name is Baldly Ken.

Ken: My hair has grown. You can simply call me Ken.

Goldy: Stop it.

Pause.

Goldy: Before I left the office this morning, I bowed to Guan Gong at the altar and said, I am ready to kill today. I will kill anyone who stands in my way to wealth. If I see God on the road, I'll hack him to pieces. If I see the Buddha, I'll hack him too…

Ken: It's not "hack".

Goldy: So, Cutting Keung…

阿強 /Ken：……

黃金：　喂老大，兩塊錢不是錢啊？我在超級市場攢了好久積分才攢到兩張，不信你撕開瞧瞧，有血有 ─

【黃金不自覺地自己把 Coupon 撕開】

阿強 /Ken：……

黃金：　（用口水粘好撕開的 Coupon）粘起來都還能用……插隊強，你當還我一個人情……

Ken：　插隊強？

黃金：　就這一次……

Ken：　你什麼時候有插隊這個習慣的？

黃金：　帶上你的拍檔，走人。

阿強：　他不是我的拍檔。

Ken：　我是他的同學。

阿強：　他叫禿頭 Ken。

Ken：　我頭髮已經長出來了，你叫我阿 Ken 就行了。

黃金：　夠了。

【靜默片刻】

黃金：　我早上離開公司之前，對關公拜了三拜，然後跟他説：「關二哥，今天我一定要大開殺界！誰他媽擋我發財我就殺誰，見神劈神，見佛劈佛……」

Ken：　不是劈。

黃金：　插隊強……

39

Ken: It should be kill.

Goldy: I've done you a lot of favours…

Ken: It should be, "If I see the Buddha, I'll kill the Buddha."

Goldy: …

Ken: All appearances are illusory.

Goldy: Last time at King's Court when thousands of warriors…

Ken: To see that appearances are not appearances is to see the Tath gata.

Goldy: Have you damn well finished?

Ken: That is to say, all visions that we see are illusory. Even if you see Buddha, it is illusory. You have to rid yourself of all these illusory appearances. Only once you do that can you see the real Buddha. This is what is meant by, "If you see the Buddha, kill the Buddha."

           Pause.

Goldy: Are you sure he was your schoolmate?

Keung: Try killing him.

Goldy: …

Keung: If you kill him, I can confirm whether he was or not.

           Pause.

Goldy: Alright.

           Goldy takes out a pistol and points it at Ken's head.

Ken: To kill the Buddha, is to see the Buddha.

           Goldy shoots.

Ken： 是殺。

黃金： 我都讓過你不少次啦⋯⋯

Ken： 是見佛殺佛。

黃金： ⋯⋯

Ken： 凡所有相，皆是虛妄。

黃金： 上次在帝皇苑千軍萬馬⋯⋯

Ken： 若見諸相非相，即見如來。

黃金： 你他媽講完了沒啊？

Ken： 意思就是說，我們肉眼所見到的一切，都是虛幻，就算你見到佛，都是虛幻，你要當看不到他，當你看不到他時候，你才可以真真正正見到佛，見佛殺佛是這個意思。

【靜默片刻】

黃金： 你肯定他是你的同學？

阿強： 你試試殺了他。

黃金： ⋯⋯

阿強： 你殺了他，我就可以確定是不是。

【靜默片刻】

黃金： 好。

【黃金拔出一支手槍，指着 Ken 的頭】

Ken： 殺佛，是為了見佛。

【槍聲】

第四場

Scene 4

Scene 4

One second immediately after the previous scene.

The three of them are in the same position. The pistol in Goldy's hand has vanished. He is pointing at Ken with his fingers.

Two more people are in the show flat. They are Eu Look and New Seeland. They are in their thirties.

The five of them stand there as if frozen in time.

After a while, Eu Look and New Seeland start to move.

Look: This living room could really welcome our guests…

Seeland: Disgusting!

Eu Look opens a door and peeps in.

Look: This bedroom could really help us fall asleep.

Seeland: Disgusting!

Eu Look opens another door and peeps in.

Look: This toilet…

Seeland: What about the toilet?

Look: Shit…

Seeland: What?

Look: It's really a toilet.

Seeland: Disgusting!

Look: But these three…

Seeland: Sculptures.

Look: Why did they put three sculptures here?

Seeland: Disgusting!

第四場

【距上場約一秒】

【三人保持先前的姿勢，不同的是，黃金手中的槍消失了，他只是用手指指着 Ken】

【單位內多了兩個人 ── 歐陸和辛西蘭，這時的他們，年約 30 餘歲】

【五個人不動，彷彿「凝結」在歷史的一刻】

【過了一會，歐陸和辛西蘭的身體開始活動】

歐陸： 這間客廳真的可以招呼客人的喔⋯⋯

辛西蘭： 太過份啦！

【歐陸打開一道門向內觀看】

歐陸： 這間睡房真的可以讓人睡得着覺的喔。

辛西蘭： 太過份啦！

【歐陸打開另一道門向內觀看】

歐陸： 這間廁所⋯⋯

辛西蘭： 怎樣啊？

歐陸： Shit⋯⋯

辛西蘭： 吓？

歐陸： 真是一間廁所來的喔。

辛西蘭： 太過份啦！

歐陸： 但是這三個⋯⋯

辛西蘭： 雕塑。

歐陸： 為什麼要擺三個這麼大的雕塑在這兒呢？

辛西蘭： 太過份啦。

Look: Is this what they mean by lifestyle choices?

Keung, Ken and Goldy move and want to speak to New Seeland at the same time. But before they can speak, New Seeland screams out loudly, like a terrified bird. The three of them are scared and lost. They stop moving.

Look: Don't be scared.

Seeland: If the sculptures in your home turned into human beings, wouldn't you be scared?

Look: My home is yours too. Why would we be so dumb as to put sculptures in our home?

Seeland: This is the core question…

Look: You mean…

Keung and the other two start to move again.

New Seeland screams out again, the three stand still then.

Seeland: They've turned into humans again.

Look: Who are you?

Ken   All appearances are illusory. To see that appearances are not appearances is to see the Tath gata.

Seeland: Is this a message from the spirits?

New Seeland takes out a pair of cymbals. Eu Look takes out a bronze bell. They play the instruments in a ritual and chant a kind of incantation.

Seeland   *Ong a mi die wa she*
/Look: *Ong bei ma da lie hong*
             Ong a mi die wa a yi si de hong she

The three men struggle to leave. Stuck like ghosts under the chanting of Look and Seeland.

歐陸： 難道這就是傳説中生活的品位？

【阿強、Ken 和黃金的身體同時活動，同時要向歐陸和辛西蘭講話，但話還未説出口，辛西蘭卻像一隻驚弓之鳥般尖叫起來。阿強等三人反被嚇得不知所措，也不敢再動】

歐陸： 別怕！

辛西蘭： 如果你房子裏有幾個雕塑，忽然變成人了，你不怕？

歐陸： 我房子不就是你房子，你房子怎麼會這麼無聊擺幾個雕像在這兒啊？

辛西蘭： 問題的癥結就在這裏⋯⋯

歐陸： 你的意思是説⋯⋯

【阿強等三人再次活動起來】

【辛西蘭再尖叫，三人再停住】

辛西蘭： 他們又變成人了。

歐陸： 來者何物？

Ken： 凡所有相，皆是虛妄。若見諸相非相，即見如來。

辛西蘭： 這些還不是靈異的訊號？

【辛西蘭拿出一對鈸，歐陸拿出一個銅鈴。兩人搖鈴擊鈸，進行某種儀式，口中唸唸有詞地唱／頌着某種咒語】

歐陸
／辛西蘭： 唵 *ong* 阿 *a* 彌 *mi* 爹 *die* 哇 *wa* 舍 *she*
唵 *ong* 唄 *bei* 瑪 *ma* 達 *da* 列 *lie* 吽 *hong*
唵 *ong* 阿 *a* 彌 *mi* 爹 *die* 瓦 *wa* 阿 *a* 依 *yi* 斯 *si* 德 *de*
吽 *hong* 舍 *she*

【三人在歐陸和辛西蘭唱／頌聲中，似三個幽靈，掙扎着退下】

第五場

Scene 5

Scene 5

Immediately following the previous scene.

Eu Look has stopped chanting, but not New Seeland.

Eu Look rings the bell.

Seeland: Oh?

Look: It's clear.

Seeland: Wow…

Look: I've asked you not to be so engaged.

Seeland: I was drawn…

Look: Restrain yourself. Keep your eyes half closed. Keep one eye on yourself and the other on them. That is how you stay in control.

Seeland: I will pull myself together if I can.

Look: How many times do I have to tell you?

Seeland: Those things are everywhere.

Look: I am well prepared in this business.

Seeland: Look…

Look: This is why I constantly tell you to always keep your tools with you.

Seeland: Are you not tired?

Look: Take a seat if you are tired.

Seeland: I mean…

Look: Let me check this flat out.

Seeland: I am going too far…

Look: The ceiling is high enough.

第五場

　　　　　　　【接上場】

　　　　　　　【歐陸停止了頌唱，但辛西蘭仍繼續】

　　　　　　　【歐陸搖鈴】

辛西蘭：　　咦？

歐　陸：　　已經打發出去啦。

辛西蘭：　　嘩……

歐　陸：　　就跟你說不用這麼投入的啦。

辛西蘭：　　他們一直扯住我……

歐　陸：　　你冷靜一點，眼睛半張半合，一半望自己，一半看他
　　　　　　們，這樣你才能控制大局嘛。

辛西蘭：　　能冷靜我早就冷靜啦！

歐　陸：　　怎麼說你都這樣。

辛西蘭：　　這幫王八蛋真是無處不在。

歐　陸：　　做這一行我早該料到啦。

辛西蘭：　　阿 Look……

歐　陸：　　所以我說像傢伙要隨身帶就是這個意思。

辛西蘭：　　你不累的嘛？

歐　陸：　　累你就坐下休息一會嘍。

辛西蘭：　　我說的是……

歐　陸：　　看完屋子再說。

辛西蘭：　　我已經快不行啦……

歐　陸：　　天花還真高。

Seeland: I can't go any farther…

Look: The floor is solid.

Seeland: I won't be able to take it if we go any farther…

Look: As high as the sky, as solid as the earth.

Seeland: Let's take this one!

           Pause.

Seeland: Look…

Look: We shouldn't be too casual…

Seeland: I am talking to you.

Look: If we are too casual, we'll pay for it our whole lives.

Seeland: I've paid my whole life already.

Look: What?

Seeland: To marry you, I have already sold it off.

Look: Oh.

Seeland: How much longer do you have to look?

Look: But you have to find the right one…

Seeland: Ten years.

Look: …

Seeland: Ten years, since you showed me the pile driver at the construction site and we have been seeing five show flats a week since then. We have seen two thousand seven hundred show flats. This is the two thousand seven hundred and first show flat. Two thousand seven hundred and first…

Look: This is not about me…

Seeland: If this is about me, then it is OK.

Look: This is about the next generation.

辛西蘭： 我撐不住啦……

歐陸： 地板也挺厚。

辛西蘭： 再下去我就要掛啦……

歐陸： 天高、地厚。

辛西蘭： 不如就這套吧！

【靜默片刻】

辛西蘭： 阿 Look……

歐陸： 我們做事千萬不能隨便……

辛西蘭： 我在跟你說話啊。

歐陸： 一隨便你就一輩子……

辛西蘭： 我已經一輩子啦。

歐陸： 吓？

辛西蘭： 嫁給你，我已經一輩子啦。

歐陸： 哦。

辛西蘭： 你還要 Look 多久啊？

歐陸： 那你也要看上眼了才 —

辛西蘭： 十年。

歐陸： ……

辛西蘭： 十年前，從你帶我去看人蓋房子打樁開始，一直到現在，我們平均每個禮拜看五個單位，一共看了 2,700 個，這是第 2,701 個，2,701 啊……

歐陸： 這個不是我一個人的事……

辛西蘭： 我整個人等於 OK 兩個字。

歐陸： 還有我們的下一代。

Seeland:	Do we need to think so far ahead?
Look:	How could we be so short sighted?
Seeland:	…
Look:	To be a responsible man, one must be responsible for the following generations. My home today is my world tomorrow.
Seeland:	Tomorrow they might live on Mars. Shall we check out the flats on Mars too?

New Seeland tries to exit.

Eu Look doesn't move.

New Seeland stops.

Seeland:	Why don't you move?
Look:	Too easily agitated. That is your problem.
Seeland:	My problem?
Look:	When you are agitated, you lose your mind.
Seeland:	OK.
Look:	I can't do anything with you like this.
Seeland:	I am very calm now and I want to say…
Look:	You say it, say it, say it.

Pause.

Seeland:	This one…
Look:	…
Seeland:	I wish for this to be the last one.
Look:	…
Seeland:	The last one…

辛西蘭： 需要想那麼遠嗎？

歐陸： 目光怎麼可以短淺的呢？

辛西蘭： ……

歐陸： 作為一個負責任的男人，我一定要為我的子孫負責，今天我的家，將來他天下……

辛西蘭： 將來他們可能已經住上火星了，不如我們現在去火星看房子吧。

　　　【辛西蘭向外走】

　　　【歐陸不動】

　　　【辛西蘭停】

辛西蘭： 你還在這裏？

歐陸： 你的問題就是容易激動。

辛西蘭： 我的問題？

歐陸： 一激動就失去理智。

辛西蘭： OK.

歐陸： 你這樣我做不了事的。

辛西蘭： 我現在很冷靜地跟你說……

歐陸： 你說啊你說啊你說啊。

　　　【靜默片刻】

辛西蘭： 這一套……

歐陸： ……

辛西蘭： 我希望是最後。

歐陸： ……

辛西蘭： 最後……

Look: …

Seeland: This one.

New Seeland exits.

Eu Look is puzzled. He rings the bell in his hand unconsciously.

The bell rings like an indication of time. It fades.

歐陸：　　……

辛西蘭：　這一套。

　　　　　【辛西蘭下】

　　　　　【歐陸有點惘然，下意識搖了一下手中的鈴】

　　　　　【鈴聲彷彿是時間的一個 Index，在慢慢退去的同時，
　　　　　時間亦被模糊了】

第六場

Scene 6

Scene 6

A corridor outside the show flat.

Time shifts back to the end of Scene 4. Keung, Goldy and Ken walk out from the show flat.

The chanting of Eu Look and New Seeland can still be heard inside the flat.

Look   *(V.O)*
/Seeland: *Ong a mi die wa she*
           Ong bei ma da lie hong
           Ong a mi die wa a yi si de hong she

The chanting acts like glue, holding Keung, Goldy and Ken in place, they have to fight to break away.

The chanting fades out.

Keung: That fucking asshole…

Goldy: It's so fucking choking…

Keung: What the fuck are they doing here in a show flat?

Goldy: Big spenders like that practice a lot.

Keung: Who is it?

Goldy: Mao Shan?

Keung: Really?

Goldy: Greedy Chan made his first fucking fortune with this practice, fuck.

Ken: Did he?

Keung   …
/Goldy:

第六場

【單位外的一條走廊】

【時間接駁第四場結束時，阿強，黃金和 Ken 從單位內出來】

【單位內仍然傳出歐陸與辛西蘭唸頌咒語的聲音 —】

歐 / 辛： （V.O.）
唵 *ong* 阿 *a* 彌 *mi* 爹 *die* 哇 *wa*　舍 *she*
唵 *ong*　唄 *bei* 瑪 *ma*　達 *da* 列 *lie*　吽 *hong*
唵 *ong* 阿 *a* 彌 *mi* 爹 *die* 瓦 *wa*　阿 *a* 依 *yi* 斯 *si* 德 *de*
吽 *hong* 舍 *she*

【這聲音像一種強力膠膜，黏着阿強，黃金和 Ken。他們以超出正常的力氣才能「撕破」膠膜羈絆】

【唸頌聲退去】

阿強： 啊我操他媽的……

黃金： 媽的差點被他搞死……

阿強： 來看樓而已嘛，需要來這套嗎？

黃金： 現在大款很他媽的喜歡搞這套的。

阿強： 這他媽是幹毛的？

黃金： 茅山，我操你媽的。

阿強： Really?

黃金： 陳振聰也是靠這玩意起家的，我日你大爺。

Ken： 能起嗎？

阿強
/ 黃金： ……

Ken: There is righteousness in the earth.

Keung   …
/Goldy:

Ken: Even if he did, he will fall soon.

Keung   …
/Goldy:

Ken: They are chanting The Song of Compassion.

Keung   …
/Goldy:

Ken: Usually it is sung for the dead on their way towards rebirth
           and to the pure land of utmost bliss.

           Ken exits.

Goldy: What the fuck is he talking about?

Keung: You're asking me?

Goldy: Is he trying to tell us he is fucking well educated and
           knowledgeable?

Keung: He is fucking well educated and knowledgeable.

Goldy: Fuck you. Why isn't he an intellectual then? What is he
           doing here?

Keung: When we met in Form One he used to recite a collection of
           Ten Thousand Questions of Life. Man, there are a hundred
           of them. He recited them until the day he graduated from
           secondary school. He was already bald.

Goldy: If he wasn't your friend, I would have punched him in his
           god-damn face.

Keung: After secondary school, I heard he went to Wudang School
           to learn Baguazhang martial arts. He killed two wolves with
           a single hand.

Ken： 天地有正氣。

阿強
/ 黃金： ……

Ken： 能起家才有鬼。

阿強
/ 黃金： ……

Ken： 他們唸的是慈悲咒。

阿強
/ 黃金： ……

Ken： 通常是唸給死人聽的，送它們去往生極樂淨土。

【Ken 下】

黃金： 他説什麼鳥啊？

阿強： 你問我？

黃金： 好像讀過很他媽多書，很他媽有知識是不是？

阿強： 他確是讀過很他媽多書、很他媽有知識啊。

黃金： 我操他媽的這麼多知識幹毛不做知識份子？來這幹鳥
啊？

阿強： 我中學一年級認識他的時候，他整天背一套書，叫做
《人生的一萬個為什麼》，他媽幾百本，他一路背到中
學畢業，頭髮都掉光了。

黃金： 如果不是你認識他，我真想幹他一頓。

阿強： 中學畢業之後，聽説他去武當山學八卦掌，一掌可以
劈死兩隻大野狼。

Goldy:	You mother fucker, one hand can only kill one. How can he possibly kill two?
Keung:	The wolves were mating.
Goldy:	…
Keung:	That's what I heard. Why don't you challenge him? I will set it up…
Goldy:	No, no, no…
Keung:	You scared?
Goldy:	We are all men. Every one of us has his own legend. It's no fucking good to expose reality, right? We should be kind.
Keung:	You mother fucker, you dare tell me to be kind?!
Goldy:	Or we can talk about my business.
Keung:	What business?
Goldy:	Last time at King's Court when thousands of warrior salesmen flocked in, I opened the road for you, I lay on the ground and let you climb your way up on my back…
Keung:	Fuck you. Last time you were scared and collapsed to the ground. There were lots of fucking people climbing up on your back…
Goldy:	But you made the deal, didn't you?
Keung:	…
Goldy:	Even if I was scared and collapsed, you still owe me a favour, don't you?
Keung:	…
Goldy:	If someone does a good deed for you, even after a thousand years you would reward him, wouldn't you?
Keung:	…
Goldy:	It's time…

黃金： 操他姥姥，一掌最多拍死一隻，他媽的怎麼拍死兩隻？

阿強： 據說那兩隻大野狼正在嘿咻。

黃金： ⋯⋯

阿強： 傳言而已嘛，不如你去試試他，我幫你跟他說⋯⋯

黃金： 不用不用不用⋯⋯

阿強： 你腿軟啊？

黃金： 大家都是男人，每個男人背後都有個神話，沒必要戳穿嘛，對不對？做人要厚道嘛。

阿強： 你個屄樣居然跟我講厚道？

黃金： 不講厚道就先回來講我的⋯⋯

阿強： 講你哪根毛啊？

黃金： 上次在帝皇苑千軍萬馬，我幫你殺開一條血路，趴在地上，給你他媽踩在我背上⋯⋯

阿強： 那次是你他媽自己腿軟撲街，他媽踩你背上的除了我還他媽有很多人。

黃金： 反正他媽你那次是搞定了，對不對？

阿強： ⋯⋯

黃金： 就算是我自己腿軟撲街，你都算是得過我的恩惠，對不對？

阿強： ⋯⋯

黃金： 滴水之恩當湧泉相報，對不對？

阿強： ⋯⋯

黃金： 這次我－

Keung: What the fuck are you trying to say?

Goldy: Fuck you…

Keung: If your client comes first, I go. If mine comes first, you go.
            OK?

Goldy: …

            Keung looks at his watch.

            Goldy looks at his watch.

            Pause.

Goldy: Where the fuck is your friend?

Keung: …

阿強： 我什麼我？

黃金： 日你妹……

阿強： 總之一句話，你客戶先到，我走，我客戶先到，你走，OK？

黃金： ……

　　　　【阿強看表】

　　　　【黃金看表】

　　　　【靜默片刻】

黃金： 你的同學他媽去哪了？

阿強： ……

第七場
Scene 7

Scene 7

Immediately after the previous scene.

In the show flat.

Ken is holding two glasses of champagne. He gives Eu Look one.

Ken: It's not the best, but it's good enough to rinse your mouth out with.

Eu Look takes the glass.

Ken takes a sip of the champagne.

Eu Look pours the champagne into a plant pot.

Look: How long have you been here?

Ken: What?

Look: Many a time I go to my homeland in dreams. Forever my gravestone will face my birthplace.

Ken: Very philosophical.

Look: I know you are reluctant to leave, I understand that completely.

Ken: May I have your name please?

Look: I am very easy going. I am fine if you don't bother me too much.

Ken: You are in a hurry?

Look: I am like you, I came to visit.

Ken: After the visit, we will follow our own paths.

Pause.

Eu Look exits.

第七場

【距上場約一秒】

【單位內】

【Ken 拿着兩杯香檳，一杯遞給歐陸】

Ken： 雖然不是什麼好貨，漱漱口還 OK 啦。

【歐陸接過酒杯】

【Ken 喝下】

【歐陸把酒倒進一個盆栽】

歐陸： 上來多久了？

Ken： 吓？

歐陸： 活着夢回故土，死後墓向原鄉。

Ken： 很有深意。

歐陸： 我知道你們捨不得，我完全理解。

Ken： 怎麼稱呼啊？

歐陸： 我這個人真的無所謂，只要別太妨礙我就行啦。

Ken： 你趕時間。

歐陸： 我跟你們一樣，都是來參觀而已。

Ken： 看完就走，各走各路。

【靜默片刻】

【歐陸走】

Ken: Maybe I can help you?

          Eu Look stops.

Look: First, help yourself.

          Ken presents his name card to Eu Look.

Ken: Helping you would indeed be helping myself.

          Eu Look takes the name card.

Ken: I am Ken.

Look: …

Ken: Your wife is visiting the Club House. Thousands of my acquaintances are serving her at the moment. There is no rush.

Look: …

Ken: Did you walk in?

Look: …

Ken: It's good to walk in. You always bump into the best flats that way.

Look: Like bumping into ghosts, right?

Ken: Almost.

Look: …

Ken: Your first buy?

Look: …

Ken: It's common.

Look: …

Ken: You have too many choices.

Look: …

Ken: If not, it's even harder.

Ken： 也許我能幫你呢？

【歐陸停】

歐陸： 先顧好你自己吧。

【Ken 遞卡片給歐陸】

Ken： 幫你不就是顧我自己囉。

【歐陸接過卡片】

Ken： 我叫阿 Ken。

歐陸： ⋯⋯

Ken： 你太太去參觀 Club house，下面招呼她的人多的是，其實不用急嘛。

歐陸： ⋯⋯

Ken： 你們 Walk in 的？

歐陸： ⋯⋯

Ken： Walk in 好啊，通常好貨都是無意碰上的嘛。

歐陸： 就像見鬼一樣，對吧？

Ken： 差不多。

歐陸： ⋯⋯

Ken： 首次置業？

歐陸： ⋯⋯

Ken： 對嘛對嘛。

歐陸： ⋯⋯

Ken： 舉棋不定嘛。

歐陸： ⋯⋯

Ken： 不是就有麻煩了。

Look: …

Ken: You have to think it over for sure. Don't let any outside factors or on site pressure influence you.

Look: …

Ken: It's not a game of clear winners.

Look: …

Ken: I've seen a lot in this business.

Look: …

Ken: Let me tell you a story…

Look: …

Ken: It's just a story, don't take it too seriously.

Look: …

Ken: There was a man called A. A was very good at his studies, very hardworking. He paid his taxes every year. He married when he was in his thirties and bought his first flat for two million dollars. But thirty years later, in order to pay the installments, he's basically stuck working for the bank. He's lost all of his dreams. Isn't that miserable?

Look: …

Ken: Eventually, in his sixties, after he's paid all the installments, the government forces all landlords to examine their buildings. The report recommends maintenance and renovation. He has to spend another hundred thousand, it hits him harder than being struck by lightning in a thunderstorm. The worst part is, he wanted to sell the flat but nobody wanted it. Finally, he ends up living on the streets with his wife. (But at the same time...)

Look: (But at the same time...)

Ken: …

歐陸： ……

Ken： 當然要想清楚啦，千萬不要受外界因素和現場壓力影響。

歐陸： ……

Ken： 買房子不一定贏的。

歐陸： ……

Ken： 我做這一行見過不少啦。

歐陸： ……

Ken： 講個故事給你聽吧……

歐陸： ……

Ken： 你當故事聽聽就算啦，千萬不要認真。

歐陸： ……

Ken： 從前有一個人，他叫 A 君，A 君讀書很牛逼，做事又勤奮，年年繳稅，30 歲就結婚，結婚後還有錢付首期，於是買了個兩百多萬的單位，但是接下來 30 年，基本上，他就為了這間房子替銀行打工，什麼夢想都沒了，你說慘不慘？

歐陸： ……

Ken： 這還不算，等他熬到 60 多歲快掛的時候，忽然間政府要強制檢驗房子，驗完之後報告拿來一看，我操！要給十多萬去維修，簡直比被雷打更慘。更慘的是，想賣掉它又沒人要，結果走投無路，兩口子流落街頭。（但是與此同時……）

歐陸： （但是與此同時……）

Ken： ……

Look	But at the same time, there is another man called B. B is not very good academically. He worked as a freelancer and got married in his thirties. The couple applied for public housing and got a flat. They took the advice of the city's Chief Executive and gave birth to as many children as possible, they applied for social security when they were unemployed and each month they got more than ten thousand dollars for their living expenses. After thirty years, their flat at the public housing estate was worn out so the government used the money from A to carry out maintenance and renovation. He enjoyed his days taking care of their grandchildren, taking in the city's scenery. When walking with his grandson one day he pointed out A who was living under a bridge and said to him, "When you grow up, remember to apply for public housing. Otherwise, you will be like that old man there."

Pause.

Ken:	That story is widely spread on the internet.
Look	Finished?
Ken:	It might be a little bit exaggerated.
Look	I think it is very realistic.
Ken:	A story like this told by a salesman of a real estate company, you must be astonished.
Look	It further affirms my beliefs.
Ken:	Your beliefs…
Look	A "human being" wouldn't talk to me like that.
Ken:	(Of course…)
Look	(Of course…)

Pause.

Look	You used to be a human.

歐陸：	與此同時有個傻 B 叫 B 君，B 君讀書不行就去打工，同樣可以在 30 歲的時候結婚，然後兩口子一齊申請公共房屋，輕易就有房住，住進去之後沒啥幹的，就聽特首建議，狂生小孩，找不到事做就申請綜援，一個月萬把塊都花不完。30 年之後，他們的公屋單位已經又殘又爛，但不要緊，因為有政府用 A 君的錢幫他們維修，沒事就帶帶孫子，閑了就去街上散步，指着天橋底的 A 君對孫子說：「看吧，以後長大了努力申請公屋啊，否則你就像這老頭一樣撲街啦。」

【靜默片刻】

Ken：	網上流傳了很久啦。
歐陸：	講完了？
Ken：	的確是有點誇張。
歐陸：	我覺得好現實喔。
Ken：	一個地產銷售跟你講一個這樣的故事，你一定覺得匪夷所思。
歐陸：	我只會更加肯定我的想法。
Ken：	你的想法是……
歐陸：	一個「人」－ 不會跟我講這些亂七八糟的。
Ken：	（那當然啦……）
歐陸：	（那當然啦……）

【靜默片刻】

歐陸：	你「曾經」是一個人。

Ken: At this stage in your life, you are prepared to struggle through hell.

Look   I understand totally.

Ken: I feel like we are communicating well.

Look   I've been in your company for far too long already. I am in a hurry…

Ken: I think there may have been a misunderstanding.

Look   Don't complicate things.

Ken: It is I who has been in your company.

Look   The fact is you're dead. There is no way to come back.

Ken: Even if I am dead, that's not a problem. I just wanted to talk about the story…

Look   There are thousands of stories in this world…

Ken: I have finished my story, but I want to add one thing…

Look   OK.

Ken: There are two men in the story. A and B.

         Eu Look heads towards the exit.

Ken: What I want to say is…

         Eu Look stops.

Ken: Apart from A and B, there are C,D,E,F,G,H,I,J,K,L,M,N, O,P,Q,R,S,T,U,V,W,X,Y and Z.

         Eu Look exits.

Ken: And you…

         Eu Look stops.

Ken: I am not sure which one you are. But one thing I can be sure of, the one who walks into this flat is neither A nor B.

Ken：　　　人生來到這一步，每天都有在地獄裏打滾的準備啦。

歐陸：　　　我完全明白。

Ken：　　　我發覺我跟你很好溝通喔。

歐陸：　　　我陪了你這麼久，都說得過去了，我還有要緊的事⋯⋯

Ken：　　　我想你有點誤會。

歐陸：　　　你不用再囉嗦啦⋯⋯

Ken：　　　應該是我陪你才對啊。

歐陸：　　　死了就是死了，沒得重生的。

Ken：　　　死不是問題，我想跟你再說之前那個故事⋯⋯

歐陸：　　　人世間，有千千萬萬個講不完的故事⋯⋯

Ken：　　　我的故事講完了，我只是想補充一句 −

歐陸：　　　OK.

Ken：　　　故事裏面有兩個人，一個是 A 君，一個是 B 君。

　　　　　　【歐陸走】

Ken：　　　我想講的是⋯⋯

　　　　　　【歐陸停】

Ken：　　　這個世界除了 A 和 B，還有 C, D, E, F, G, H, I, J, K, L, M, N, O, P, Q, R, S, T, U, V, W, X, Y 和 Z⋯⋯

　　　　　　【歐陸走】

Ken：　　　而你⋯⋯

　　　　　　【歐陸停】

Ken：　　　我不知道你是哪個，但有一點我可以肯定，走得進這個單位的，一定不會是 A 和 B⋯⋯

	Eu Look exits.
Ken:	And you…
	Eu Look stops.
Ken:	From the moment you walked into this flat, I could tell you wouldn't be easy to define as one of the twenty four letters…
	Eu Look heads towards the exit again.
Ken:	And I…
	Eu Look stops.
Ken:	What I want to add is that…
Look	…
Ken:	You have gone beyond the twenty six letters.
Look	…
Ken:	What you are looking for is not a flat or a house. You are looking for a home. A home, is your occupied area. First you occupy a home, and next you occupy the world. That is uniting heaven and earth.
Look:	…

【歐陸走】

Ken： 而你⋯⋯

【歐陸停】

Ken： 由你第一步走進來，我就看得出，就算用餘下的 24 個英文字母，即是 C, D, E, F, G, H, I, J, K, L, M, N, O, P, Q, R, S, T, U, V, W, X, Y 和 Z，都 Define 不到你⋯⋯

【歐陸走】

Ken： 而我⋯⋯

【歐陸停】

Ken： 我要補充這一句就是⋯⋯

歐陸： ⋯⋯

Ken： 在住這個問題上面，你已經超越了 26 個英文字母。

歐陸： ⋯⋯

Ken： 你要找的不是一間房子，不是一間套房，你要找的是一個家。家，其實是一個佔領區，由家出發，你要佔領天下，即是家天下。

歐陸： ⋯⋯

第八場
Scene 8

Scene 8

10 minutes immediately after the previous scene.

Somewhere in the show flat – It can be a balcony, a bedroom etc. – We will take it as a balcony for the sake of ease of description.

New Seeland, Keung and Goldy are on the balcony.

New Seeland is wearing wavy clothes. Goldy kneels down on the floor controlling a fan which is facing Seeland. Keung plays the violin.

New Seeland is pondering over something.

The theatre transforms into a huge grassland scene.

Seeland: *(Sings The Beautiful Grassland is my home.)*
The beautiful grassland is my home.
The wind blows over the green grass and flowers.
Colourful butterflies fly and hundreds of birds sing.
Clear water reflects the sunset's glow.
Beautiful horses run like rolling clouds.
Cows and sheep scattered like pearls.
Oh, shepherd women sing out loud.
Songs of happiness are everywhere.
Oh, shepherd women sing out loud.
Songs of happiness are everywhere.

New Seeland stops singing.

Pause.

Goldy: It's almost perfect, right?

Seeland: …

Keung: In that case, why don't we…

Seeland: I want to take a look at the sea view please.

第八場

【距上場約十分鐘】

【單位的某個部分 ── 可能是一個陽台，也可能是一間睡房，諸如此類……為了方便陳述，且稱此處為陽台吧】

【陽台裏有辛西蘭，阿強和黃金】

【此時的辛西蘭穿着一件飄逸的衣服，黃金蹲在地上，操控着一把風扇吹向辛西蘭，阿強在一旁拉小提琴】

【辛西蘭似在凝思】

【劇場裏漸顯草原景象】

辛西蘭：　(唱：《美麗的草原，我的家》)
　　　　　美麗的草原我的家
　　　　　風吹綠草遍地花
　　　　　彩蝶紛飛百鳥兒唱
　　　　　灣碧水映晚霞
　　　　　駿馬好似彩雲朵
　　　　　牛羊好似珍珠撒
　　　　　啊，牧羊姑娘放聲唱
　　　　　愉快的歌聲滿天涯
　　　　　啊，牧羊姑娘放聲唱
　　　　　愉快的歌聲滿天涯

【辛西蘭唱完】

【靜默片刻】

黃金：　　差不多了吧。

辛西蘭：　……

阿強：　　既然已經差不多了，不如我們 ─

辛西蘭：　來個海景吧，謝謝。

Goldy: What?

Seeland: In a South Pacific Islands style. Do you have one?

Keung: Sure, we do.

            Keung takes out a menu.

Keung: *(To Goldy)* position 26.7, channel 22.

            Goldy shifts the fan to a different position. He takes a remote control and pushes it in the direction of Keung. Keung plays his violin in a South Pacific Islands style.

            The theatre transforms into a South Pacific Islands scene.

Seeland: The desert, please.

Goldy: What?

Seeland: Gobi Desert. Can you do that?

Keung: 38.6, 25.

            Goldy repeats his previous action. Keung plays accordingly.

            The theatre transforms into a Gobi Desert scene.

Seeland: Niagara Falls.

Keung: 16.2, 12.

            Goldy follows.

            The theatre transforms into a Niagara Falls scene.

Seeland: Grand Canyon… Great Barrier Reef… Jiuzhaigou Valley… Rocky Mountains… Golden Bauhinia Square…

            The command from New Seeland goes quicker and quicker. Goldy and Keung can hardly follow. The changing scenes become chaotic.

            The scene in the theatre gradually transforms into a cemetery.

黃金： 吓？

辛西蘭： 南太平洋島嶼 Feel，不知道有沒有呢？

阿強： 有，一定有。

【阿強拿出一份 Menu 查看】

阿強： （對黃金）Position 26.7，Channel 22.

【黃金調較風扇，移動方位，再拿出一個遙控器，向阿
強按了一下，阿強的演奏隨即變成「南太平洋島嶼」
風格】

【劇場裏漸顯「南太平洋島嶼」景象】

辛西蘭： 沙漠，謝謝。

黃金： 吓？

辛西蘭： 大戈壁沙漠，有沒有啊？

阿強： 38.6、25。

【黃金重複剛才步驟，阿強的演奏相應改變】

【劇場漸顯「大戈壁沙漠」景象】

辛西蘭： 尼加拉瓜瀑布。

阿強： 16.2、12。

【黃金跟進】

【劇場裏漸顯「尼加拉瓜瀑布」景象】

辛西蘭： 大峽谷……大堡礁……九寨溝……洛磯山脈……金紫
荊廣場……

【辛西蘭的指令愈來愈急，黃金與阿強亂作一團，劇場
裏的「景象」亦顯得一片混亂】

【劇場裏混亂的景象漸變成「墳場」】

Seeland: Wow! That is enough. Stop it.

              Keung and Goldy stop.

Goldy: We can keep going.

Seeland: We will end up in hell if we keep going.

Keung: Don't worry Mrs Eu. With me, Keung, there is only one place you will end up. Heaven.

Seeland: Heaven is not my destination, and don't call me Mrs. I am not used to it. You can simply use my English name.

Goldy: Your English name is…

Seeland: Seeland.

Keung: What?

Seeland: Seeland. My family name is New.

Goldy: New Seeland?

Seeland: New Seeland.

Keung: I don't like to brag, but every single person that walks into this flat is very special in their own way. Even their names are unique.

Seeland: Every one of us has a unique name?

Goldy: But none dare to call themselves New Seeland.

Keung: That's why I said you "clicked" with this flat. See? The flat is open enough for us to see in its entirety, inside and out.

Goldy: Let's talk about the product I just introduced…

Keung: The product we introduced.

Goldy: What do you think about it?

Seeland: What was it called again?

辛西蘭： 嘩！行了行了，不用再來啦。

【阿強與黃金停下】

黃金： 其實我們還可以繼續的。

辛西蘭： 再來就下地獄啦。

阿強： 你放心吧歐太太，有我阿強在這兒，你只有一條路走，就是上天堂。

辛西蘭： 天堂也不是我的目的地，By the way，我不是太習慣被人叫太太，你叫我英文名就行啦。

黃金： 你的英文名是……

辛西蘭： Sai-lan（粵音「晒冷」）。

阿強： 什麼？

辛西蘭： 就是西蘭，我姓辛。

黃金： 辛西蘭？

辛西蘭： Sai-lan Sun.

阿強： 真的不是我阿強喜歡拍馬屁，進得來這個單位的，果然連名字都不同凡響。

辛西蘭： 每個人的名字都不同的啦。

黃金： 但沒人夠膽子叫自己「晒冷」的嘛（編劇按：粵語「晒冷」的意思是把自己最強勢的一面展示人前 — 即示威）。

阿強： That's why 我説這個單位跟你合拍，杠杠的，see？整間房子，由內到外，基本上就是用來「晒冷」的。

黃金： 先回來説一下我之前跟你介紹的那個產品吧……

阿強： 是我們一起介紹。

黃金： 你試過之後覺得怎樣啊？

辛西蘭： 叫什麼名字來着？

Keung: /Goldy:	Window to the World.
Seeland:	That's amazing.
Keung:	The whole package goes with the flat.
Goldy:	3-D World Window fan.
Keung:	Digital violin.
Goldy:	Optical fibre remote control.
Keung:	And the dress you are wearing.
Goldy:	The whole package goes with the flat.
Keung:	Basically, the violin and the 3-D fan are programmed. All you have to do is select where you want to go and press the button…
Goldy:	Take a look at the menu…
Keung:	Everything is included.
Goldy:	You can change the scenery as you like…
Seeland:	With only one button?
Keung /Goldy:	With only one button.
Seeland:	The possibilities are endless…
Keung /Goldy:	*Sing the theme song The World is Under my Feet of a TV drama called Qin Shi Huang.* *With the land trembling under my feet,* *The whole of the empire in my hands,* *Who dares to say a single word to offend me?* *Having vanquished the six states and built my empire,* *I have attained what no one has ever attained!* *On top of everyone, I order you to behold:* *My empire is as stunningly beautiful as the best paintings!* *Up on the mountaintop and surrounded by clouds,*

阿強
/ 黃金：　　世界之窗。

辛西蘭：　　挺神奇的嘛。

阿強：　　　整套都是送的。

黃金：　　　3-D 風扇。

阿強：　　　數碼提琴。

黃金：　　　光纖遙控。

阿強：　　　包括你現在穿的這條裙。

黃金：　　　整套都是送的。

阿強：　　　Basically，這個數碼提琴和這架 3-D 風扇已經 Program 了，你只要找對按鈕，一按就行了……

黃金：　　　你看這份 Menu……

阿強：　　　應有盡有……

黃金：　　　隨時都可以換景……

辛西蘭：　　只要我按一個按鈕？

阿強
/ 黃金：　　只要你按一個按鈕。

辛西蘭：　　然後就無邊無際……

阿強
/ 黃金：　　*(唱：電視劇「秦始皇」主題曲《大地在我腳下》)*
　　　　　　大地在我腳下　國計掌於手中　哪個再敢多説話
　　　　　　夷平六國是誰　哪個統一稱霸　誰人戰績高過孤家
　　　　　　高高在上　諸君看吧　朕之江山美好如畫
　　　　　　登山踏霧　指天笑罵　捨我誰堪誇
　　　　　　秦是始　人在此　奪了萬世瀟灑
　　　　　　頑石刻　存汗青　傳頌我如何叱吒

I dare even to scold the heavens, and boast my insurmountable accomplishments.
The First Emperor is here, my line will continue forever and ever.
The stone tablets I erected. The history books will trumpet this greatest Emperor of all times.

Seeland: Wonderful… wonderful…

Goldy: I knew you knew that…

Seeland: But there is something… missing.

Keung: If it was me singing the song a capella, it would have been totally different…

Goldy: The gravity of it would have been lost.

Keung: You were not singing the song. You were raping the song.

Seeland: No, no, no, no. I am not talking about you. Your performance was wonderful. Impeccable. I am talking about… the Window of the World.

Goldy: Aren't there enough scenes for you?

Keung: The software can always be upgraded.

Seeland: No, I am talking about the mood.

Keung /Golden: …

Seeland: No matter what scenery you introduced, my mood was still the same. It didn't change.

Keung: That means…

Seeland: Grasslands, waterfalls, oceans, valleys, deserts, they were all the same.

Goldy: The question is…

Seeland: The mood and the scenery don't "click".

辛西蘭：　　Wonderful…wonderful…

黃金：　　　這就叫做識貨的……

辛西蘭：　　但是好像還有……有點欠缺。

阿強：　　　剛才如果由我一個人獨唱的話，就會完全不同了……

黃金：　　　完全沒有皇者氣派了嘛。

阿強：　　　你剛剛不是唱歌，你是在強姦這首歌。

辛西蘭：　　No, no, no, no！我不是說你們，你們的表演真的Wonderful，無懈可擊。我說的是……世界之窗。

黃金：　　　你是不是覺得景點不夠？

阿強：　　　軟件方面隨時都可以 Upgrade。

辛西蘭：　　我講的是心情。

阿強
/ 黃金：　　……

辛西蘭：　　之前無論轉去什麼景點，我的心情始終都是一樣，沒有改變。

阿強：　　　也就是說……

辛西蘭：　　草原、瀑布、大海、峽谷、沙漠，全部一樣。

黃金：　　　這個問題是……

辛西蘭：　　情和景，不能融合在一齊。

Pause.

Keung: Let's try it again.

Seeland: I've seen enough.

Goldy: Failure is the mother of success.

Seeland: It's time to find your colleague.

Keung: Ken?

Goldy: He is serving Mr Eu.

Seeland: Go and pick him up now. Three come. Three go. Keep a constant team. Come back next time when you are free.

Keung: Mrs Eu…

Seeland: Don't call me Mrs Eu…

Goldy: Seeland, we have had the luck to meet each other after a hundred years…

Seeland: I know it's rare…

Keung: Hold on hold on… *(To Goldy)* Please take your hundred years back…

Goldy: What do you mean?

Keung: *(To New Seeland)* I was talking to you just now. *(To Goldy)* I haven't finished. *(To New Seeland)* Why is he putting a hundred years into our conversation?

Seeland: I don't know.

Goldy: It was I who first talked to her, Cutting Keung.

Seeland: Cutting Keung?

Keung: Please don't use my nickname in front of my client! That is really unprofessional!

Goldy: Your client? How can you say she is your client? Did you make an appointment with her? *(To New Seeland)* Seeland, did he make an appointment with you?

【靜默片刻】

阿強：　不如我們再試一次。

辛西蘭：　夠了。

黃金：　失敗乃成功之母。

辛西蘭：　是時候回去找你們那個隊友了。

阿強：　阿 Ken ？

黃金：　他好像在招呼歐先生喔。

辛西蘭：　你們現在去接他，三個來、三個走；齊齊整整，整理好隊形，有空再上來玩。

阿強：　歐太太……

辛西蘭：　都說不要叫我太太嘛……

黃金：　「晒冷」，今天我跟你百年難得一遇 —

辛西蘭：　我也知道很難得……

阿強：　等一下等一下……（對黃金）你這一百年麻煩收回去……

黃金：　什麼意思？

阿強：　（對辛西蘭）我剛才在跟你講話，（對黃金）我還沒說完呢，（對辛西蘭）他突然插一百年進來幹嘛呢？

辛西蘭：　我不知道啊。

黃金：　是我先跟她說話的，插隊強！

辛西蘭：　插隊強？

阿強：　在我的客戶面前，請你不要叫我的花名！你很不專業啊！

黃金：　你客戶？！你憑什麼說她是你的客戶啊？！你約他來的嘛？（對辛西蘭）晒冷，是他約你來的嗎？

Seeland: You don't usually make any appointments for this kind of thing.

Goldy: *(To Keung)* She said no.

Keung: Oldy Goldy!

Goldy: What?

Keung: Is this the way you work?

Goldy: This has always been my way.

Keung: Good.

Goldy: It's good.

Seeland: Let's go.

Keung: You dare show my land?

Seeland: What?

Goldy: I dare to show your land.

Seeland: You two…

Goldy and Keung take out pistols.

The sound of a gunshot.

Black out.

Lights up.

Seeland is stuck to something, such as a wall, perhaps the ceiling or something equally absurd. She appears to have been blown back by a strong force.

Keung and Goldy remain in the same position as before the black out. But they are not holding pistols. Instead they are clenching their fists. They are about to play a multiplication game.

Keung: Five…

辛西蘭： 你們這種「東西」一般都沒得約的喔。

黃金： （對阿強）沒有啊。

阿強： 黃老金！

黃金： 幹嘛？

阿強： 你是不是這麼幹？

黃金： 我一向都這麼幹。

阿強： 好。

黃金： 好就行了。

辛西蘭： 行就走吧。

阿強： 你現在跟我「晒冷」是吧？

辛西蘭： 吓？

黃金： 我現在是跟你「晒冷」。

辛西蘭： 兩位……

【黃金與阿強拔出手槍】

【槍聲】

【燈滅】

【燈亮】

【辛西蘭「貼」在某處或某物 － 例如牆上、天花等，愈離奇愈好……彷彿剛才被一股強大的力量迫彈成這樣】

【阿強與黃金保持燈滅前的姿勢，但手中沒有拿槍，他們握着的是「拳頭」，是「猜枚」的「拳頭」－ 他們在「猜枚」】

阿強： 五……

Goldy: Ten…

Keung: Fifteen…

Goldy: Seeland!

Keung: Twenty five…

Goldy: Thirty…

Keung: Seeland!

Keung and Goldy improvise the numbers they shout out and throw in the occasion "Seeland." Gradually, they take out the numbers, they are only saying "Seeland."

Seeland gradually pulls herself away from whatever she was stuck to.

Seeland: Hey man, is that enough?

Keung and Goldy continue with the game. They shout out "Seeland" occasionally.

Seeland: I only came here to see the show flat. You don't need to take it so seriously.

Keung and Goldy continue.

Seeland: Everything has a procedure. You can't rush these things…

Keung and Goldy continue.

Seeland: Give me some time to check it out. If it is alright and I decide to buy it, I will be sure to reward you…

Keung and Goldy continue.

Seeland: Alright, wherever I move, before I move in, I will prepare a massive feast, invite all the Taoist Priests, monks, nuns and lamas, including Greedy Chan. I will perform a traditional religious ceremony to release you and send you off in peace. Your spirits will live free forever. Is that enough?

Keung and Goldy continue.

黃金：	十……
阿強：	十五……
黃金：	晒冷！
阿強：	二十五……
黃金：	三十……
阿強：	晒冷！

【他們所唱的數字是即興的，其間也即興地加插一聲「晒冷」，漸漸地，他們把數字隱去，只剩下動作和間斷的「晒冷」之聲】

【辛西蘭慢慢把身體「撕」離所「貼」之處或物】

辛西蘭： 喂老大，玩夠了吧？

【阿強和黃金持續猜枚動作和「晒冷」之聲】

辛西蘭： 我來看房子而已，你們不用搞得這麼嚴重吧。

【阿強和黃金持續】

辛西蘭： 幹什麼都要講程序嘛，急不來的嘛老大……

【阿強和黃金持續】

辛西蘭： 你們多給我一點時間，等我看完，滿意，要買了，我自然會處理的了……

【阿強和黃金持續】

辛西蘭： 總之無論我搬去哪兒，在我入伙之前，我一定會請人來，道士、和尚、施姑、喇嘛、陳振聰我都幫你們請出來，做場大戲，給你們好好瞧瞧，安安樂樂，浩氣長存，這樣行不行啊？

【阿強和黃金持續】

Seeland:	That is enough!
	Keung and Goldy stop.
Seeland:	I am only looking for a place for human beings to live in. Is that too much to ask?
	Keung and Goldy freeze.
Seeland:	I am a human being! I am not dead yet! I still have my human rights!
	Keung and Goldy freeze.
Seeland:	What is the most basic human right?
	Keung and Goldy freeze.
Seeland:	To live in a place suitable for a human being!
	Pause.
Seeland:	You can't even understand the basics. How can you be an efficacious ghost? Pu-le-a-mo!
	Keung and Goldy exit.
Seeland:	Sorry… I am sorry… I shouldn't be so emotional. I am not prejudiced against you. I understand the pathetic situation that drove you to this state. But… I am pathetic too… Can't you try to understand my situation?
	Keung and Goldy re-enter.
Goldy:	No problem…
Seeland:	Oh?
Keung:	We are listening…
Seeland:	Again?
Goldy:	As always…
Seeland:	Hey man…

辛西蘭： 夠啦！

【阿強與黃金靜止】

辛西蘭： 我只不過是想找一個「人」住的地方，不算很過份對不對？

【阿強與黃金不動】

辛西蘭： 我是人來的！我還沒死的！我有人權的！

【阿強與黃金不動】

辛西蘭： 一個人最基本的人權是什麼啊？！

【阿強與黃金不動】

辛西蘭： 是住在一個適合「人」住的地方啊！

【靜默片刻】

辛西蘭： 這麼簡單的道理都不明白，你們還怎麼做鬼啊！幹！

【阿強與黃金退下】

辛西蘭： Sorry…I am sorry…我不應該這麼激動，我對你們真的沒有成見，我知道你們好慘，走投無路才淪落到這種地步。但是……我也很倒楣啊老大……你們可不可以嘗試了解一下我啊？

【阿強與黃金重上】

黃金： 沒問題……

辛西蘭： 咦？

阿強： 一直在聽……

辛西蘭： 又來？

黃金： 永遠守候……

辛西蘭： 喂老大……

Keung:	Just say it…
Seeland:	What?
Goldy:	I was born to understand you…
Seeland:	Really?
Keung:	Just tell me.
Seeland:	Me?
Goldy:	Seeland…
Seeland:	You…
Keung:	What's your problem?
Seeland:	What?
Goldy:	Anything concerning living can be resolved.
Seeland:	I…
Keung:	You haven't got any place to stay?
Seeland:	No.
Goldy:	That means you have.
Seeland:	If you say so.
Keung:	Improving ones living conditions is a common wish shared by all human beings.
Seeland:	I'm glad you understand it.
Goldy:	Moving into a more spacious place makes one happier.
Seeland:	I live in a place with ten thousand square feet of space.
Keung /Goldy:	What?
Seeland:	Full of maids.

阿強： 你講就行啦……

辛西蘭： 吓？

黃金： 我老媽生我出來，就是來了解你……

辛西蘭： 不是吧？

阿強： Just tell me。

辛西蘭： 我？

黃金： 「晒冷」……

辛西蘭： 你……

阿強： What's your problem？

辛西蘭： 吓？

黃金： 只要是住的問題都可以解決。

辛西蘭： 我……

阿強： 你現在沒房住嗎？

辛西蘭： 不是。

黃金： 不是就是有啦。

辛西蘭： 也可以這麼説。

阿強： 改善居住環境，是人類普遍的願望。

辛西蘭： 你知道就最好啦。

黃金： 換一個寬敞一點的地方，人都會開朗好多。

辛西蘭： 我現在住的地方有上萬呎。

阿強
/ 黃金： 吓？

辛西蘭： 滿屋都是丫環。

Keung /Goldy:	Oh.
Seeland:	Together with slaves, mistresses, acquaintances, there are two to three hundred of them.
Keung /Goldy:	What?
Seeland:	Aeroplanes, cannons, steamships, everything you can think of.
Keung /Goldy:	Oh.
Goldy:	Handbags, clothes and shoes from luxurious brands are hanging everywhere.
	Pause.
Keung:	What do you do?
Seeland:	Gift supply.
Goldy:	What a large business.
Seeland:	For funerals.
Keung /Goldy:	What?
Seeland:	A paper model shop.
Keung /Goldy:	Oh.
Seeland:	In fact, it's more like a space museum.
Keung /Goldy:	What?
	Time flows like a meandering river, carrying Keung and Goldy away like ghosts.

阿強 / 黃金：	啊。

辛西蘭： 還有奴隸、二奶、小三，前前後後起碼都有二、三百個。

阿強 / 黃金：	吓？

辛西蘭： 飛機、大炮、輪船，什麼都有。

阿強 / 黃金：	啊。

辛西蘭： 手袋、衣服、鞋襪，件件都是名牌，掛得滿屋都是。

【靜默片刻】

阿強： 你家做什麼買賣的？

辛西蘭： 禮品供應。

黃金： 果然是大茶飯。

辛西蘭： 專供陪葬。

阿強 / 黃金：	吓？

辛西蘭： 就是紙紮舖。

阿強 / 黃金：	啊。

辛西蘭： 其實更像一間太空館。

阿強 / 黃金：	吓？

【時間好像一條被扭曲的河流，載着阿強及黃金，像兩隻幽靈般，漸漸退下】

第九場

Scene 9

Scene 9

Immediately after the previous scene. But time is rewound to ten years ago.

New Seeland is moving with difficulty among different kinds of paper models that hang from the ceiling. She moves like a spaceman.

Eu Look enters. He is reading a book.

Look: *Ong, hong, xi, di, suo, ha…* those who recite this song will get love and respect from heaven and earth. He will make everyone happy, make one's dreams come true, make things whole…

Seeland: Look…

Look: Oh, what are you doing?

Seeland: I just went to the toilet and can't get back.

Look: You are not young anymore. Don't play around like a child. I've got a lot to do. Go to bed.

Seeland: I am in space now. I can't feel the gravity. It's terrible.

Look: Can you be less illusionary? We should be more realistic, step by step. If you want to go to space, I will take you there one day. But not now. Come down.

Seeland: I can't. I feel like I've fallen into a big ball pool. I have no strength left.

Look: You are out of control. I've asked you not to think so much.

Seeland: I didn't think of anything. I just went to the toilet. How could I have known the toilet had turned into a space station? The earth disappeared when I walked out. Please get me down.

Look: It wasn't me who put you up there. You flew there yourself. I can't help you.

第九場

【緊接上場，但時間已倒流至約十年前】

【辛西蘭在一堆從天花吊下來的各式各樣的紙紮物當中極艱難地移動，似太空漫步】

【歐陸上，拿着一本書，邊行邊讀】

歐陸：　　唵 ong　吽 hong　悉 xi 地 di　梭 suo　哈 ha ⋯⋯常持誦此咒，得一切天人愛敬降伏，能令一切人見者歡喜，能成就一切心願，悉皆圓滿⋯⋯

辛西蘭：　阿 Look⋯⋯

歐陸：　　哇，你在這兒幹嘛啊？

辛西蘭：　我剛剛撒完夜尿，回不了頭啊？

歐陸：　　你人不小了，別玩這麼幼稚的東西啦，我還有好多事要做，去睡吧。

辛西蘭：　我飄到了太空，整個人都沒重量了，超難受啊。

歐陸：　　你別這麼虛幻行不行啊？做人要踏實點，一步一步慢慢來，你要上太空我將來一定會帶你上，但是現在還不是時候，下來吧。

辛西蘭：　我下不來啊，好像跌進了一個好大好大的波波池，使不上勁啊。

歐陸：　　這不就是失控囉，叫你不要想這麼多啦。

辛西蘭：　我沒多想啊，我只是去撒尿，我怎麼知道廁所會變成太空站？一走出來地球就不見了，你快點把我弄下來啦。

歐陸：　　現在不是我把你搞上去的，是你自己飄上去的，我幫不了你啊。

Seeland:	There is a lot of space rubbish here. I am becoming a part of it.
Look:	You are not rubbish. Hong Kong people are not rubbish.
Seeland:	Stop talking. Do something.
Look:	Alright, listen to this…
Seeland:	What's that?
Look:	The Song of *Peace on Earth*.
Seeland:	Quick.
Look:	*(Chanting)*

O the God of all gods, we beg you to order all the gods and deities,
To be on their guard, and be prepared to protect your worshippers,
In order that our mind and body are cleansed and purified, and
We return to the way of virtue, and enjoy peace and fortune.

Time flies as Eu Look chants.

辛西蘭： 這裏有好多太空垃圾啊，我都快變成垃圾啦。

歐陸： 你不是垃圾，香港人不是垃圾。

辛西蘭： 別説了，快做點什麼。

歐陸： 好吧，試一下這首吧⋯⋯

辛西蘭： 是什麼？

歐陸： 安土地咒。

辛西蘭： 快。

歐陸： （誦讀）元始安鎮，普告萬靈，嶽瀆真官，土地祇靈，左社右稷，不得妄驚，回向正道，內外澄清，各安方位，備守壇庭，太上有命，搜捕邪精，護法神王，保衛誦經，皈依大道，元亨利貞。

【時間在歐陸的誦讀聲中流轉】

111

第十場
Scene 10

Scene 10

Time shifts to the present.

Keung, Ken and Goldy gather in a corridor.

Goldy: So…

Keung: Fuck.

Pause.

Goldy: *(To Ken)* Hey man, what do you think?

Ken: My name is Ken.

Goldy: Your name is not important. I am asking your opinion. We share the commission. Each of us gets one third of it. What do you think?

Ken: I got it.

Goldy: *(To Keung)* He got it. That means he has no problem with it…

Keung: Go ahead and make the deal if you can.

Goldy: Hey…

Keung: Annex the whole fucking commission. It's a good deal.

Goldy: Hey Cutting Keung…

Keung: You can't take it all?

Goldy: Can you stop speaking to me this way?

Keung: I am very greedy.

Goldy: Are we still discussing this?

Keung: Three, Three, Four.

Goldy: What?

Keung: *(To Ken)* Three, *(To Goldy)* Three, *(To himself)* Four.

第十場

【時間回到當下】

【阿強，Ken 和黃金聚在一條走廊上】

黃金： 我……

阿強： 操。

【靜默片刻】

黃金： （對 Ken）那誰，你怎麼看？

Ken： 我叫阿 Ken。

黃金： 你的名字不重要，我是問你的意見，一人一份，分三份，你怎麼看？

Ken： 我明白。

黃金： （對阿強）他明白就是沒意見……

阿強： 有本事你他媽自己搞定它囉。

黃金： 我……

阿強： 一個人他媽獨吞掉，多好啊。

黃金： 插隊強……

阿強： 啃不動啊？

黃金： 你是這樣跟我講話的嗎？

阿強： 我食量很他媽大的喔。

黃金： 沒得商量嗎？

阿強： 三三四。

黃金： 什麼？

阿強： （指 Ken）三、（指黃金）三、（指自己）四。

Goldy: You mother fucker…

Keung: Forget about it.

Goldy: You always have to take advantage.

Keung: It's fine with me.

Goldy: I've known you for so long…

Keung: Don't say that to me.

Goldy: *(To Ken)* Hey man, say something. Why do the two of us get three while he gets four?

Ken: My name is Ken.

Goldy: I am asking for your opinion. Can you stop telling me your name? Your name is not an opinion.

Ken: I got it.

Goldy: He got it. That means he agrees with me…

Keung: I don't give a shit.

Goldy: Listen to me…

Keung: Have you said enough? What else do you want to say? That's all for me. Three, three, four. Take it or leave it. Take it and we fight together. Leave it and you leave me alone. Let me tell you, I have my style, my style is blindness. My pistol has no eyes. It shoots as it wants. You'd better take care.

            Keung starts to exit.

Goldy: Brother Keung.

            Keung stops.

Goldy: Let's be rational…

Keung: You dare to ask me to be rational?

Goldy: It doesn't help to be impetuous…

黃金：　　我去你姥爺的……

阿強：　　那就算。

黃金：　　什麼事你他媽都要佔一點便宜。

阿強：　　It's fine with me.

黃金：　　我認識你這麼久……

阿強：　　別他媽跟我說這些。

黃金：　　（對 Ken）那誰，你給點意見，你說吧，有什麼理由你三我他四呢？

Ken：　　我叫阿 Ken。

黃金：　　我叫你給意見啊！你別他媽再跟我說名字好不好？你的名字不是意見來的。

Ken：　　我明白。

黃金：　　他明白就是同意我的觀點……

阿強：　　I don't give a shit.

黃金：　　你先聽我說完……

阿強：　　媽逼你講完沒？媽逼還有什麼好說的？媽逼我就這麼分，三三四，行就一起進去，我走在前面，你們殿後，媽的打死就算，不行你就別他媽理我。But let me tell you, I have my style, my style is 盲目，我的槍什麼都不瞄，就他媽亂掃，你們顧好自己吧。

【阿強欲下】

黃金：　　強哥。

【阿強停步】

黃金：　　我們理性一點……

阿強：　　你跟我談理性？

黃金：　　這件事衝動沒用的……

Keung:	Your company is falling apart and you dare to ask me to be rational?
Goldy:	Don't talk about the company. Let's talk about us…
Keung:	Have you used up your Fairwood coupon? Do I have to save some more points for you?
Goldy:	How about Qi?
Keung:	What?
Goldy:	Qi, the one who looks like Shu Qi?
Keung:	…
Goldy:	How long have you wanted to date her? You like her. Why don't you see her?
Keung:	It's none of your fucking business.
Goldy:	It's because apart from local Hong Kong style restaurants, you dare not go anywhere else.
Keung:	Fuck you!
Goldy:	OK. Don't get emotional. Let's be rational, OK?
	Pause.
Goldy:	We are here, what for?
Keung:	…
Goldy:	Money. That's all.
Keung:	…
Goldy:	*(To Ken)* Hey man, do you agree?
Ken:	What?
Goldy:	*(To Keung)* He said what, that means…
Ken:	My name is Ken.
Goldy:	*(To Ken)* Is your name more important than money, fuck you?

阿強：　　　你公司快要破產了，你跟我談理性？

黃金：　　　不要談公司，談個人……

阿強：　　　大快活的 Coupon 用完沒有？要不要我幫你存點積分啊？

黃金：　　　阿淇怎樣啊？

阿強：　　　什麼？

黃金：　　　阿淇啊，你那個疑似舒淇的阿淇啊？

阿強：　　　……

黃金：　　　你多久沒約過她了？你喜歡她，為毛你不約她啊？

阿強：　　　關你屌事啊？

黃金：　　　因為除了茶餐廳，任何餐廳你都不敢進去。（編劇按：香港的「茶餐廳」賣的一般都是比較廉價的食物）

阿強：　　　Fuck you！

黃金：　　　OK，我們不要這麼情緒化，談回理性，OK？

【靜默片刻】

黃金：　　　進這扇門，為毛啊？

阿強：　　　……

黃金：　　　錢，講完。

阿強：　　　……

黃金：　　　（對 Ken）那誰，你同不同意？

Ken：　　　吓？

黃金：　　　（對阿強）他「吓」的意思就是 —

Ken：　　　我叫阿 Ken。

黃金：　　　（對 Ken）現在是錢重要還是你的名字重要啊我日你？

Ken: …

Goldy: Shall we be realistic?

Ken: …

Goldy: How long have you been in this business? Do you know what the golden 45 minutes is? If your client doesn't show up after 45 minutes of the appointment time, you can declare him dead. He is fucking dead. He will not show up. My client is fucking dead. Will yours be reborn?

Ken: …

Goldy: *(To Keung)* How about you? Where is your Mr Leung? Brother Keung!

Keung: …

Goldy: It's lost. The last bullet today is shot. It's shot into the black hole. It's disappeared. Total silence.

Ken/Keung: …

Goldy: Now, the two people in there just happened to walk in. If you see the Buddha, kill him. Today, this day, three, the three of us, whether we win or lose, we still win or lose… Do you understand?

Ken/Keung: …

Goldy: OK.

Ken/Keung: …

Goldy: I'll say it again… To play safe, you suggest using both a horizontal and vertical strategy. Unify those conflicting elements into a solid, conquering power. Unleash the dominant position. Win the biggest victory. Share the largest interests.

Ken: What you mean is: Together, we will win together. Separate, we will lose together. That's it.

Goldy: …

Ken：　　……

黃金：　　現實一點行不行？

Ken：　　……

黃金：　　你什麼時候入行的？你知不知道什麼叫黃金 45 分鐘？當你的客戶遲到超過 45 分鐘，你就可以宣布他掛了，他已經嗝屁啦，他不會再出現啦，我的客戶已經嗝屁啦，你的客戶會活過來嗎？

Ken：　　……

黃金：　　（對阿強）你呢？你的梁先生去哪兒了？強哥！

阿強：　　……

黃金：　　不會來啦，今天唯一的一顆子彈已經用掉了，打進個鳥黑洞裏面，銷聲匿跡，聲音都他媽聽不到了。

Ken／阿強：……

黃金：　　現在，裏面那兩個鬼使神差走了進來。總之，見神劈神，見佛劈佛。今天，就在今天，三個，我們三個，輸了一起輸、贏了一起贏……你們明不明白我說什麼？

Ken／阿強：……

黃金：　　OK.

Ken／阿強：……

黃金：　　我再說一遍，作為一種相對安全的戰略，我建議採用合縱連橫的模式，將所有互相矛盾的敵對成份，統合成為一股堅實的征服力量，發揮最大優勢，爭取最大勝利，分享最大利益……

Ken：　　你的意思是說，合 — 就三個一起贏；分 — 就三個一起輸，說完。

黃金：　　……

Ken: In fact, it's just one word: Encircle.

Goldy: …

Ken: It's like hunting. Encircle the animals. Close all the exits. Narrow down the scope, until they have no way out. This way, we can take them one at a time. Break their necks. Tear their stomachs open. Rip out their guts. Let the blood run thick.

           Pause.

Goldy: You are talking about dogs.

Ken: Yes.

           Pause.

Ken: Hunting dogs.

           Pause.

Goldy: Are we hunters?

Ken: How can we be hunters?

Goldy: …

Ken: Those who build are hunters. We are just hunting dogs.

Goldy: …

Ken: My name is Ken.

Goldy: …

Ken: Baldly Ken.

           Ken takes out a piece of paper.

Ken: Here is the plan.

Goldy
/Keung: …

Ken: If you are interested in joining me, then we are friends.

Ken： 其實就一個字：圍。

黃金： ⋯⋯

Ken： 就像打獵一樣，圍住野獸打，封住所有出口，然後慢慢收窄範圍，等他們走投無路，最後一口一隻，吃下去，咬斷他脖子、撕開他肚子、腸子扯出來、放乾他的血。

　　　　【靜默片刻】

黃金： 你說得好像狗一樣。

Ken： 是啊。

　　　　【靜默片刻】

Ken： 獵狗嘛。

　　　　【靜默片刻】

黃金： 我們不是獵人嗎？

Ken： 我們怎麼會是獵人呢？

黃金： ⋯⋯

Ken： 蓋樓的那些才是獵人，我們只是獵狗而已。

黃金： ⋯⋯

Ken： 我叫阿 Ken。

黃金： ⋯⋯

Ken： 禿頭 Ken。

　　　　【Ken 拿出一張紙】

Ken： 這裏有個 Plan。

黃金
/ 阿強： ⋯⋯

Ken： 有興趣一起來搞，不就是 Friend 了嗎？

123

Keung: What's this?

Ken: Trial Residency.

Goldy: A trial package?

Keung: I have never heard of it.

Ken: It's not too late to hear about it.

阿強： 什麼來的？

Ken： Trial Residency.

黃金： 試住套餐？

阿強： 沒聽過。

Ken： 現在聽也不晚。

第十一場

Scene 11

Scene 11

Ten minutes after the previous scene.

Inside the show flat.

Eu Look and New Seeland are in casual wear.

Eu Look sits on the sofa. He's trembling and twitching.

Look: Oh… yo… yi… ya…

Seeland: How's that?

Look: Oh…

Seeland: Can you stop talking so abstractly?

Look: It's like I'm being hit by a thousand arrows…

Seeland: Really?

Look: Piercing my heart…

Seeland: Let me try…

Look: Here, here…

New Seeland sits down on the sofa. She trembles and twitches as well.

Seeland: Wow…

Look: Isn't it great?

Seeland: I feel like I'm being…

Look: Woo…

Seeland: Torn apart…

Look: Aya…

Seeland: Into pieces…

Look: All into pieces…

第十一場

【時間距上場約十分鐘】

【示範單位內】

【歐陸和辛西蘭穿着家居便服】

【歐陸坐在梳化上，全身顫抖，不時抽搐】

歐陸：　　噢……yo……咿……ya……

辛西蘭：　幹嘛？

歐陸：　　啊……

辛西蘭：　可不可以別這麼抽象？

歐陸：　　萬箭穿心……

辛西蘭：　這麼嚴重？

歐陸：　　心如刀割……

辛西蘭：　讓我也試試……

歐陸：　　這裏這裏……

【辛西蘭坐下沙發，身體亦隨之顫抖及抽搐起來】

辛西蘭：　嘩……

歐陸：　　爽不爽啊？

辛西蘭：　好像被人……

歐陸：　　Woo……

辛西蘭：　劈開……

歐陸：　　啊……

辛西蘭：　一節一節……

歐陸：　　全部劈碎……

Seeland:	Here…
Look:	There…
Seeland:	Disgusting…
Look:	Disgusting…

Both of them stop trembling and twitching suddenly.

Seeland:	Uh?
Look:	It's over?
Seeland:	Didn't they say two hours?

Eu Look takes out a piece of paper and reads.

Look:	Trial Residency, duration: two hours. Massage sofa in service for three minutes.
Seeland:	It can't be true?
Look:	It's written on the plan.
Seeland:	It just tore me apart, now they have to put me back together.
Look:	*(Examining the sofa)* Which brand is it?
Seeland:	It would be good if it lasted three minutes longer…
Look:	*(Reading out the sofa brand)* Dreaming in a Dream?
Seeland:	Three more minutes, I would be in heaven…
Look:	Have you heard of it?
Seeland:	What?
Look:	I am asking if you've heard of this brand.
Seeland:	What brand?
Look:	Dreaming in a Dream.
Seeland:	Oh…

辛西蘭： 東一節……

歐陸： 西一節……

辛西蘭： 太過份啦……

歐陸： 太過份啦……

【兩人忽然停止顫抖 / 抽搐】

辛西蘭： 咦？

歐陸： 這麼快就玩完了？

辛西蘭： 還說兩小時？

【歐陸拿出一張紙看】

歐陸： 整體試住時間兩小時，沙發按摩功能局部供應三分鐘。

辛西蘭： 不是吧？

歐陸： 這 Plan 是這麼寫的。

辛西蘭： 剛剛才進入狀況，這麼快就完了？

歐陸： （研究沙發）什麼牌子來的……

辛西蘭： 如果可以再 Last 多三分鐘就好了……

歐陸： （讀沙發牌子）「夢中有夢」？

辛西蘭： 三分鐘，簡直升仙都行啊……

歐陸： 你有沒有聽過啊？

辛西蘭： 吓？

歐陸： 我問你有沒有聽過這個牌子啊。

辛西蘭： 什麼牌子啊？

歐陸： 「夢中有夢」。

辛西蘭： 啊……

Pause.

Look: Seeland?

Seeland: Yes?

Look: Are you dreaming?

Seeland: I wish I were.

Look: A dream should be realised, not dreamt about.

Seeland: How long did you say the Trial Residency lasted?

Look: Two hours.

Pause.

Seeland: The time left is…

Look: More than an hour.

Pause.

Seeland: Time flies, doesn't it?

Pause.

Seeland: Life is like a dream.

Pause.

Seeland: Dreaming is unimportant. It only matters whether it becomes a reality.

Pause.

Seeland: A real dream.

Pause.

Look: If…

Seeland: …

Look: I say if…

Seeland: …

【靜默片刻】

歐陸：　　「晒冷」？

辛西蘭：　吓？

歐陸：　　你在做夢？

辛西蘭：　我也想。

歐陸：　　夢想是用來實現的，不是用來做的。

辛西蘭：　你之前說試住的時間是……

歐陸：　　兩小時。

　　　　　【靜默片刻】

辛西蘭：　現在剩下的時間是……

歐陸：　　一小時。

　　　　　【靜默片刻】

辛西蘭：　時間過得真快啊。

　　　　　【靜默片刻】

辛西蘭：　好多東西都像做夢一樣。

　　　　　【靜默片刻】

辛西蘭：　我覺得做夢不要緊，要緊的是真實。

　　　　　【靜默片刻】

辛西蘭：　一場真實的夢。

　　　　　【靜默片刻】

歐陸：　　如果……

辛西蘭：　……

歐陸：　　我只是說如果。

辛西蘭：　……

Look: If we buy this flat.

Seeland: You mean you will not buy it?

Look: I said "If we buy this flat".

            Pause.

Look: If we buy this flat, and we live together thereafter…

Seeland: You mean we will separate?

Look: Can you stop misinterpreting my words like that?

Seeland: …

Look: "If", is just conjecture.

Seeland: …

Look: If you and I…

Seeland: …

Look: We have…

Seeland: Thirty years.

Look: OK. Assume we will live for thirty years…

Seeland: Are you sure that's OK?

Look: What?

Seeland: Is it too long?

Look: You suggested it.

Seeland: So you do think it is too long.

Look: That's not what I meant.

            Pause.

Look: If you…

歐陸：　　如果我們買下這套房。

辛西蘭：　你的意思是你不會買？

歐陸：　　我是説「如果我們買下這套房」。

【靜默片刻】

歐陸：　　如果我們買下這套房，一直都是住在一起 —

辛西蘭：　你的意思是我們會分手？

歐陸：　　你別這樣曲解我的想法好不好？

辛西蘭：　……

歐陸：　　「如果」，只不過是一個假設。

辛西蘭：　……

歐陸：　　假設我跟你……

辛西蘭：　……

歐陸：　　我跟你還有……

辛西蘭：　30 年。

歐陸：　　OK，假設我們還有30 年命 —

辛西蘭：　真是 OK ？

歐陸：　　吓？

辛西蘭：　30 年不會太長嗎？

歐陸：　　是你説的嘛。

辛西蘭：　那你就是覺得太長了嘛。

歐陸：　　我不是這個意思啊。

【靜默片刻】

歐陸：　　如果你 —

Seeland: OK.

Look: …

Seeland: We will live for thirty years.

Look: …

Seeland: So?

Pause.

Look: For the next thirty years.

Seeland: You and I.

Look: We will live in this flat.

Seeland: Like now.

Look: …

Seeland: What's wrong with that?

Look: I'm sorry.

Seeland: No, no, no…

Look: I'm too serious.

Seeland: Not really.

Look: I think too much.

Seeland: You are making assumptions.

Look: I'm glad you understand.

Seeland: Actually, I don't understand.

Pause.

Seeland: I really don't understand.

Pause.

辛西蘭：　OK.

歐陸：　……

辛西蘭：　我們還有 30 年命。

歐陸：　……

辛西蘭：　怎樣呢？

　　　　　【靜默片刻】

歐陸：　未來 30 年。

辛西蘭：　我跟你。

歐陸：　都住在這套房裏。

辛西蘭：　就像現在一樣。

歐陸：　……

辛西蘭：　有什麼問題呢？

歐陸：　I'm sorry.

辛西蘭：　No, no, no…

歐陸：　我太過嚴肅了。

辛西蘭：　不會啊。

歐陸：　我想得太遠了。

辛西蘭：　都說如果而已嘛。

歐陸：　幸好你明白。

辛西蘭：　其實我不明白。

　　　　　【靜默片刻】

辛西蘭：　我真的不明白。

　　　　　【靜默片刻】

Seeland:	What do you want?
Look:	Calm down.
Seeland:	I'm sorry.
Look:	No, no, no…
Seeland:	I will control my emotions.
Look:	You are getting better.
Seeland:	So what do you want to say? Say it while I am in control.
	Pause.
Seeland:	Please.
Look:	For the next thirty years, I don't want us to live in… a mortuary.
	Pause.
Seeland:	Mortuary.
Look:	I know it might be my problem.
Seeland:	A mortuary.
Look:	But I do have this feeling…
Seeland:	How interesting.
Look:	Before a deceased person can be placed in a coffin, we put makeup on them…
Seeland:	Thirty years.
Look:	A show flat is the same. Every inch of it is decorated, made up, renovated, transformed…
Seeland:	The next thirty years.
Look:	Every time I enter a show flat, I feel as though I've walked into a mortuary…
Seeland:	You are only mentioning this now?

辛西蘭：　你到底想……？

歐陸：　　冷靜。

辛西蘭：　I'm sorry.

歐陸：　　No, no, no…

辛西蘭：　我會控制我的情緒。

歐陸：　　已經進步了。

辛西蘭：　那到底你想說什麼呢？你說啊，在我還能控制我情緒
　　　　　的時候，你把話說完。

　　　　　【靜默片刻】

辛西蘭：　Please.

歐陸：　　我不想未來 30 年，我跟你，住在一套……停屍房裏面。

　　　　　【靜默片刻】

辛西蘭：　停屍房。

歐陸：　　我知這可能是我的問題……

辛西蘭：　一套停屍房。

歐陸：　　但我真有這種感覺……

辛西蘭：　蠻有趣的嘛。

歐陸：　　一個人死了之後，要經過化妝才能入殮……

辛西蘭：　30 年。

歐陸：　　一個示範單位也一樣，每一寸都經過修飾，化妝，甚
　　　　　至改裝，改造……

辛西蘭：　未來 30 年。

歐陸：　　每次來看房都有這種感覺，好像進了一間停屍房……

辛西蘭：　你現在才說？

Look:	I only now understand.
Seeland:	I see.
Look:	Don't be emotional.
Seeland:	Don't worry.
Look:	I think communication is very important.
Seeland:	It's not the first day I've known you.
Look:	There are things I couldn't express before.
Seeland:	I've been living in the paper model shop with you for half of my life *(Takes out a remote control and presses a button).*
Look:	I keep asking myself...
	The theatre transforms, the scenery becomes mysterious.
Look:	What's this? What's this?
Seeland:	Hell.
Look:	What?
	New Seeland takes out a violin.
Seeland:	The next stop after the mortuary, is hell.
	New Seeland starts to play the violin.
	The show flat scene transforms into purgatory.
Look:	Wow...
	New Seeland continues to play.
Look:	When did you learn how to do that?
	New Seeland continues to play.
Look:	Don't be emotional...
	New Seeland continues to play.

歐陸：　　　我現在才明白。

辛西蘭：　　原來是這樣。

歐陸：　　　你別激動。

辛西蘭：　　別傻啦。

歐陸：　　　我覺得溝通很重要。

辛西蘭：　　我第一天認識你嗎。

歐陸：　　　有些東西我以前說不出是什麼。

辛西蘭：　　紙紮舖我都跟你住了大半輩子了。（拿起遙控，按）。

歐陸：　　　我天天都問自己……

　　　　　　【劇場裏漸顯「詭異」景象】

歐陸：　　　是什麼呢？是什麼東西呢？

辛西蘭：　　地獄啊。

歐陸：　　　吓？

　　　　　　【辛西蘭拿起小提琴】

辛西蘭：　　停屍房之後，是地獄啊。

　　　　　　【辛西蘭演奏小提琴】

　　　　　　【示範單位顯現「煉獄」景象】

歐陸：　　　嘩……

　　　　　　【辛西蘭繼續演奏】

歐陸：　　　你什麼時候學會這玩意的？

　　　　　　【辛西蘭繼續演奏】

歐陸：　　　你真的別激動……

　　　　　　【辛西蘭繼續演奏】

Look:	Try to be detached…
	New Seeland continues to play.
Look:	What I want to say is…
	New Seeland continues to play.
Look:	It's a concept.
	New Seeland continues to play.
Look:	Living is a concept.
	New Seeland continues to play.
Look:	Every concept has a holistic meaning.
	New Seeland continues to play.
Look:	I just want to clarify this meaning. Can you stop playing?!
	New Seeland continues to play.
Look:	We can't talk if you continue like this!
	New Seeland continues to play.
	Eu Look picks up the intercom.
Intercom:	*(V.O.)* Show flat temporary service centre. What can I do for you?
Look:	The Yin force is very strong here.
Intercom:	*(V.O.)* What?
Look:	Can you do something about it?
Intercom:	*(V.O.)* Um…
Look:	Can you?
Intercom:	*(V.O.)* Sure.
	New Seeland plays Blood Stained Glory.

歐陸： 你試試抽離點……

【辛西蘭繼續演奏】

歐陸： 我想說的是……

【辛西蘭繼續演奏】

歐陸： 是一個概念。

【辛西蘭繼續演奏】

歐陸： 「住」，是一個概念。

【辛西蘭繼續演奏】

歐陸： 任何概念，都有一個完整的含意。

【辛西蘭繼續演奏】

歐陸： 我只不過是想搞清楚這個含意你可不可以停一下啊？！

【辛西蘭繼續演奏】

歐陸： 你這樣我們是談不了的！

【辛西蘭繼續演奏】

【歐陸拿起桌上（或牆上）的 Intercom】

Intercom：（V.O.）示範單位臨時服務處，請問有什麼可以幫你？

歐陸： 這裏陰氣好重。

Intercom：（V.O.）吓？

歐陸： 你們能不能找人來清理一下？

Intercom：（V.O.）嗯……

歐陸： 可不可以啊？

Intercom：（V.O.）馬上來。

【辛西蘭奏出《血染的風采》】

Ken, Keung and Goldy enter. They are dressed as Liu Bei Ken, Guang Yun Chang Keung and Zhang Fei Goldy. They sing Blood Stained Glory.

Perhaps I'll bid farewell, never to return.
Can you comprehend? Do you understand?
Perhaps I will fall, never to rise again.
Do you still want to wait forever?
If it's to be like this, don't be sad.
The flag of the Republic has our blood-stained glory.
If it's to be like this, don't you be sad.
The flag of the Republic has our blood-stained glory.
Perhaps my eyes will shut and never open again.
Will you understand my suppressed emotions?
Perhaps I will sleep forever, never able to wake up.
Will you believe that I have transformed into mountains?
If it's to be like this, don't you be sad.
The land of the Republic contains the love we have given.
If it's to be like this, don't you be sad.
The land of the Republic contains the love we have given.
If it's to be like this, don't you be sad.
The flag of the Republic has our blood-stained glory.
If it's to be like this, don't you be sad.
The flag of the Republic has our blood-stained glory.
Blood-stained Glory.

After they finish the song, they form into a traditional sculpture of Liu Bei, Guang Yun Chang and Zhang Fei. See the following picture as a reference.

【Ken，阿強和黃金上，分別裝扮成劉備（Ken）、關雲長（強）和張飛（金），唱着《血染的風采》】

也許我告別，再不能回來，
你是否理解，你是否明白
也許我倒下，將不再起來，
你是否相信，我化做了山脈
如果是這樣，你不要悲哀，
在我們的旗幟上有我們血染的風采
如果是這樣，你不要悲哀，
在我們的旗幟上有我們血染的風采
也許我的眼睛，再不能睜開，
你是否理解我沉默的情懷
也許我倒下，再不能醒來，
你是否相信，我化做了山脈
如果是這樣，你不要悲哀，
在我們的土壤里有我們付出的愛
如果是這樣，你不要悲哀，
在我們的土壤里有我們付出的愛
如果是這樣，你不要悲哀，
在我們的旗幟上有我們血染的風采
如果是這樣，你不要悲哀，
在我們的旗幟上有我們血染的風采
血染的風采

【Ken 等三人唱完歌，集結成一個傳統的「劉關張」雕塑組合】

第十二場

Scene 12

Scene 12

Three minutes after the previous scene. Everyone is still in the same position.

Look: Can you get rid of them?

Seeland: I didn't bring them here.

Look: Are you saying it was me?

Seeland: Of course it was.

Look: Come on…

Seeland: It was you who said the Yin force was strong here. It was you who asked someone to do something about it.

Look: This is important…

Seeland: We have enough sunlight now.

Eu Look picks up the intercom.

Seeland: It's splendid.

Intercom: *(V.O.)* Show Flat Temporary Service Centre.

Seeland: It's designed like a luxurious flat.

Intercom: *(V.O.)* What can I do for you?

Seeland: I think it's OK.

Eu Look hangs up.

Look: When did you become so defensive?

Seeland: Do you even know me?

Look: I just want to clarify my thoughts with you.

Seeland: I am listening.

Look: Our problem, is a problem between you and I. I don't want anyone else involved.

第十二場

【距上場約三分鐘，單位內眾人保持着上場完結時的姿勢】

歐陸： 你可不可以把他們弄走啊？

辛西蘭： 不是我把他們弄進來的。

歐陸： 不是你難道是我？

辛西蘭： 當然啦。

歐陸： Come on⋯

辛西蘭： 剛剛你説這裏陰氣重，是你叫人來清理一下的。

歐陸： 我們正討論一些很重要的問題⋯⋯

辛西蘭： 現在夠陽光啦。

【歐陸再拿起 Intercom】

辛西蘭： 還很有氣派呢。

Intercom：（V.O.）示範單位臨時服務處。

辛西蘭： 整個就是一套豪宅啊。

Intercom：（V.O.）請問有什麼可以幫你？

辛西蘭： 我覺得 OK 喔。

【歐陸放下 Intercom】

歐陸： 你什麼時候變得這麼 Defensive 的？

辛西蘭： 你今天才認識我嗎？

歐陸： 我只是想跟你講清楚一些我的想法。

辛西蘭： 我一直在聽。

歐陸： 我們的事，是我跟你，我和你之間，我不想有其他人。

Seeland: Are you sure they are people?

Look: …

Seeland: Looking at these three quasi-human beings, all of a sudden, I get a feeling…

Look: …

Seeland: I'm starting to question whether things I used to be sure were real may in fact only be quasi-realistic.

Look: What are you trying to say?

Seeland: Truth.

Look: When have I ever deceived you?

Seeland: You haven't deceived me but that doesn't mean I know the truth.

Look: You've lost me.

Seeland: Make it clear.

Look: I can't talk to you with these things here.

Seeland: It's only for about an hour.

Look: The impact of an hour is equivalent to thirty years for us.

Seeland: Thirty years is just an assumption.

             Pause.

Look: We have nothing else to say?

Seeland: Why?

Look: OK…

Seeland: In the next hour we have to talk about everything, including all the "assumptions" and "what ifs." We have to clarify what's on your mind, your plans and your thoughts. And also your concepts, concepts, your concepts, you…

辛西蘭： 你肯定他們是人？

歐陸： ……

辛西蘭： 看着這三個疑似人類，忽然間，我開始懷疑……

歐陸： ……

辛西蘭： 我懷疑我曾經認為是真實的一些東西，其實通通都只不過是疑似真實。

歐陸： 你到底想跟我説什麼啊？

辛西蘭： 真實。

歐陸： 我有騙過你嗎？

辛西蘭： 你沒騙過我，不等於我知道真實。

歐陸： 你搞得我好混亂啊。

辛西蘭： 講清楚就行啦。

歐陸： 有這些東西在這兒，我很難跟你談下去。

辛西蘭： 不過一個多小時而已。

歐陸： 這一個多小時的影響，是我跟你的 30 年啊。

辛西蘭： 30 年，不過是一個假設而已。

【靜默片刻】

歐陸： 就是説你不想談了？

辛西蘭： 為什麼不啊？

歐陸： OK.

辛西蘭： 在這一個多小時裏面，任何東西都要談，包括所有的「假設」還有「如果」，更加要談得清清楚楚，一就一、二就二。你想怎樣？你有什麼打算？你有什麼想法？你有什麼概念？概念啊，你的概念啊，你 −

Look:	Agitation.
	Pause.
Look:	Your problem is still…
Seeland:	Excuse me.
	Pause.
Look:	*(To New Seeland)* Let's get back to your problem…
Keung:	Don't move!
	Pause.
Keung:	This is called being professional!
	Pause.
Keung:	Professional means…
	Pause.
Ken:	Sustainable.
	Pause.
Look:	Your problem is…
Ken:	Put the knife down.
	Keung feels pain. The hand holding the knife twitches.
Goldy:	What's wrong with you?
Ken:	He is twitching.
Goldy:	What?
Look:	*(To New Seeland)* Getting so easily agitated has always been your problem.
	Keung twitches so furiously that his hand holding the knife starts to move uncontrollably, dangerously, he becomes threatening. Ken and Goldy try to stop him.

歐陸：	激動。

【靜默片刻】

歐陸：	你的問題仍然是……
黃金：	Excuse me.

【靜默片刻】

黃金：	我可不可以換個姿勢啊？

【靜默片刻】

歐陸：	（對辛西蘭）說回你的問題－
阿強：	別動！

【靜默片刻】

阿強：	專業就是一個字……

【靜默片刻】

Ken：	撐。

【靜默片刻】

歐陸：	你的問題是－
Ken：	把刀放下。

【阿強好像經歷着某種痛苦，提着青龍偃月刀的手抽搐】

黃金：	你幹嘛啊？
Ken：	他抽筋。
黃金：	吓？
歐陸：	（對辛西蘭）你的問題仍然是激動。

【阿強的手被抽搐支配，不僅不能放下關刀，而且更舞動起來，險象環生，Ken 與黃金合力制止他】

New Seeland and Eu Look continue.

Seeland: I want to talk about you.

Look: There's nothing wrong with me.

Seeland: Your concept.

Look: It's very simple…

Seeland: The meaning of your concept.

Look: Listen to me…

Seeland: What does it mean?

Look: I am talking about…

Seeland: Mortuary?

Look: It is just a metaphor.

Seeland: You said this flat feels like a mortuary.

Look: Calm down.

Seeland: What do you mean by mortuary?

Look: Be rational.

Seeland: What concept?

Look: Don't get agitated.

Seeland: Say it?

Look: How can I talk to you now? You are so agitated

Ken and Goldy finally stop Keung.

【與此同時，辛西蘭與歐陸的對話繼續】

辛西蘭： 我現在想談的是你。

歐陸： 我沒問題。

辛西蘭： 你的概念。

歐陸： 好簡單……

辛西蘭： 概念裏面的含意。

歐陸： 你聽我説……

辛西蘭： 你有什麼含意啊？

歐陸： 我講的是……

辛西蘭： 停屍房？

歐陸： 只是一個比喻。

辛西蘭： 你説這套房像停屍房？

歐陸： 冷靜。

辛西蘭： 停屍房是什麼含意啊？

歐陸： 理性。

辛西蘭： 什麼概念啊？

歐陸： 不要激動。

辛西蘭： 你講啊？

歐陸： 你現在這麼激動，我怎麼跟你談啊？

【Ken 和黃金終於止住了阿強的「失控」】

第十三場

Scene 13

Scene 13

A minute after the previous scene.

Keung has calmed down. His hand holding the knife is in spasm. His fist is clenched around the knife.

Keung: (*Sings*) My brother's slain, yet their murderers are at large,
O my sworn brothers, my dearest brothers
Emaciated as I am, my head is always high
My searing hatred will keep burning till I die

Oh…

Keung is in pain.

Keung: Yin force should never be neglected. I felt it as soon as I stepped into this flat. (*To Eu Look and New Seeland*) But don't worry, ouch…

Keung is in pain.

Keung: We will call upon the mightiest of powers to get rid of the Yin force, ouch…

Keung is in pain.

Keung: (*To Ken*) My dear brother! The world is in a mess. We can't go back. We have to win this battle! Ouch…

Keung is in pain.

Keung: (*To Goldy*) Dear little brother, there are thousands of warriors like Cao Cao waiting for us outside. We can't put it off any longer. We will be killed unless we act now! Ouch…

Keung is in pain.

Keung: We can do what others do. We can even do what ghosts do. That is our gift. Let's do something about it. Ouch…

Keung is in pain.

第十三場

【距上場約一分鐘】

【阿強已平復過來，但他握青龍偃月刀的手仍在痙攣狀態，緊扣着刀】

阿強： （唱）*江左仇心空切齒，桃園義重苦傷情，幾根傲骨支床臥，一點雄心至死明*，啊⋯⋯

【阿強好像感到很痛苦】

阿強： 陰氣這種玩意兒可不是開玩笑的，剛才我一進來就中招了，（對歐陸和辛西蘭）但是你們不必擔心，啊⋯⋯

【阿強好像感到很痛苦】

阿強： 我們會燃燒最大的能量，將這間房子的陰氣，全部迫出去，啊⋯⋯

【阿強好像感到很痛苦】

阿強： （對 Ken）大哥！如今天下大亂，我們已經退無可退了。這一仗，我們一定要贏！啊⋯⋯

【阿強好像感到很痛苦】

阿強： （對黃金）三弟，外面有成千上萬個曹操等着我們，不能再猶疑了，再猶疑就會滅亡啦，啊⋯⋯

【阿強好像感到很痛苦】

阿強： 人做的事我們做得到，鬼做的事我們一樣做得到，這就是我們的優勢，動手吧，啊⋯⋯

【阿強好像感到很痛苦】

Keung: Do something about it. Ouch…

Keung is in pain.

Keung: Alright, I will take care of it on my own.

Keung inhales the Yin force.

Keung: Ouch…

Keung collapses.

Goldy goes to check him but Ken signals for him not to.

Keung gets up slowly.

Ken: If no one walks with you for the rest of your life, you have to adapt to loneliness.

Keung: Ouch…

Keung collapses.

New Seeland wants to check him out. Ken signals her not to.

Keung gets up slowly again.

Ken: If no one helps you for the rest of your life, you have to struggle alone.

Keung: Ouch…

Keung collapses.

Eu Look wants to check him out. Ken signals him not to.

Keung gets up slowly again.

Ken: When you shed no more tears, you'd better stay tough.

Keung: Ouch…

Keung collapses.

All of them want to check him out. Ken signals them not to.

Keung doesn't move anymore.

阿強：　　動手吧，啊……

【阿強好像感到很痛苦】

阿強：　　好，我一個人把它吸光。

【阿強深呼吸】

阿強：　　啊……

【阿強倒下】

【黃金欲上前關注阿強，Ken 示意他不要動】

【阿強撐起】

Ken：　　如果沒有人陪你走一輩子，你要適應孤獨。

阿強：　　啊……

【阿強倒下】

【辛西蘭欲上前關注阿強，Ken 示意她不要動】

【阿強再撐起】

Ken：　　如果沒有人幫你一生，你要奮鬥一世。

阿強：　　啊……

【阿強倒下】

【歐陸欲上前關注阿強，Ken 示意他不要動】

【阿強再撐起】

Ken：　　當眼淚流盡的時候，剩下來的，應該是堅強。

阿強：　　啊……

【阿強倒下】

【眾人欲上前關注阿強，Ken 示意他們不要動】

【阿強不再動】

Ken: Life is like a cup of black coffee. When drinking it, it tastes bitter. But even when it's gone there remains a long lasting… fragrance.

Keung doesn't move.

Goldy: Have you got any more to say?

Ken: Get him out of here.

Ken: *(To Eu Look and New Seeland)* We have removed the Yin force from the show flat. Enjoy.

Ken exits.

Ken： 人生，就像一杯沒有加糖的咖啡，喝起來是苦澀的，但是，有久久不會散去的……餘香。

【阿強仍然不動】

黃金： 你還有沒有什麼要說的？

Ken： 把他拖出去。

【黃金拖阿強下】

Ken： （對歐陸及辛西蘭）這個單位的陰氣，已經被我們消滅光了，兩位請慢用。

【Ken 下】

第十四場

Scene 14

Scene 14

A minute after the previous scene.

Eu Look and New Seeland are still in the show flat.

Look: It worked.

Seeland: What?

Look: The Yin presence has gone, the air is warm, the show flat is back to normal.

Seeland: You mean…

Look: There is true essence in heaven and earth. Apart from the true essence, there are the Yin and Yang forces. The Yin force comes from earth and the Yang force comes from heaven…

Seeland: That's enough.

Look: Yin and Yang have the same origin…

Seeland: I have had enough.

Look: Without Yang, Yin cannot stand. Without Yin, Yang cannot be independent.

Seeland: Shall we talk about us?

Look: …

Seeland: The tension between you and me.

Look: We don't need to.

Seeland: Yes we do.

Look: It's resolved.

Seeland: Not yet.

Look: It's resolved.

Seeland: Not yet.

第十四場

【距上場約一分鐘】

【單位內只有歐陸和辛西蘭】

歐陸：　　還真可以喔。

辛西蘭：　可以什麼啊？

歐陸：　　陰氣淡了、空氣暖了，整個單位 — 爽了。

辛西蘭：　你說的是……

歐陸：　　天地有正氣，正氣之外，還有陰氣和陽氣。陰氣者，地氣也；陽氣者，天氣也……

辛西蘭：　夠了。

歐陸：　　天地陰陽，本出一氣……

辛西蘭：　我真的受夠了。

歐陸：　　陽失則陰不能獨成，陰失則陽不能獨化……

辛西蘭：　不如回來說一下我跟你。

歐陸：　　……

辛西蘭：　我跟你的問題 —

歐陸：　　不要說了。

辛西蘭：　一定要。

歐陸：　　解決了。

辛西蘭：　還未解決。

歐陸：　　解決啦。

辛西蘭：　還未解決。

Look:	This one.
Seeland:	What?
Look:	It's this one.
Seeland:	…
Look:	OK?
Seeland:	…
Look:	I believe they are human beings.
Seeland:	…
Look:	Only human beings twitch.
Seeland:	…
Look:	Those in the spirit world feel pain, are tormented, defecate and have stomach-aches but they don't twitch.
Seeland:	…
Look:	No one knows the spirit world better than I do.
Seeland:	…
Look:	That's it.
Seeland:	…
Look:	This one.
Seeland:	…
Look:	The last one.
Seeland:	…
Look:	The last one.
Seeland:	…
Look:	This one.

歐陸： 就這間。

辛西蘭： 什麼？

歐陸： 就這間。

辛西蘭： ⋯⋯

歐陸： OK ？

辛西蘭： ⋯⋯

歐陸： 我想他們應該是人類。

辛西蘭： ⋯⋯

歐陸： 只有人類才會抽筋。

辛西蘭： ⋯⋯

歐陸： 靈界的物體可以有痛苦、有煎熬，甚至屙、嘔、肚子痛，但是不會有抽筋。

辛西蘭： ⋯⋯

歐陸： 沒人比我更熟悉靈界。

辛西蘭： ⋯⋯

歐陸： 就這樣了。

辛西蘭： ⋯⋯

歐陸： 這間。

辛西蘭： ⋯⋯

歐陸： 最後。

辛西蘭： ⋯⋯

歐陸： 最後。

辛西蘭： ⋯⋯

歐陸： 這間。

Seeland:	…
Look:	OK?
Seeland:	…
Look:	Well if…
Seeland:	…
Look:	This is the last "if"…
Seeland:	…
Look:	If they are human beings, we sign the contract right away and pay cash. We move in tonight, OK? Not tomorrow.
Seeland:	…
Look:	What's the matter?
Seeland:	…
Look:	If you are excited, you don't have to hide it.
Seeland:	I do think this flat is nice.
Look:	Ten years!
Seeland:	The living room will really show our hospitality.
Look:	We've been looking for ten years!
Seeland:	The bedroom would really help us sleep.
Look:	It's incredible!
Seeland:	The toilet…
Look:	Shit…
Seeland	The toilet really is a toilet.
Look:	This is what people call hunting in worn out shoes…
Seeland:	Thanks to…

辛西蘭：　……

歐陸：　　OK？

辛西蘭：　……

歐陸：　　如果……

辛西蘭：　……

歐陸：　　這是最後一個「如果」……

辛西蘭：　……

歐陸：　　如果他們真是人的話，馬上簽約，馬上付款。Cash，今晚就搬進來，明天都不用等，OK？

辛西蘭：　……

歐陸：　　怎樣啊？

辛西蘭：　……

歐陸：　　興奮，是不需要隱藏的。

辛西蘭：　我真的覺得這個單位不錯。

歐陸：　　十年！

辛西蘭：　客廳可以招呼客人。

歐陸：　　整整找了十年！

辛西蘭：　睡房可以讓人睡得着覺。

歐陸：　　簡直難以想像！

辛西蘭：　廁所……

歐陸：　　Shit…

辛西蘭：　真是廁所。

歐陸：　　這不就叫做踏破鐵鞋無覓處……

辛西蘭：　得來全靠—

171

Look:	Liu, Guan, Zhang!
	Pause.
Seeland:	Say it again.
Look:	Hunting in worn out shoes…
Seeland:	Thanks to
Look:	Liu, Guan, Zhang
	Pause.
Seeland:	Haha.
Look:	You're laughing at last.
Seeland:	Hahaha…
Look:	Stop.
Seeland:	…
Look:	Move back, give me some space.
	New Seeland moves.
Look:	Good!
	New Seeland stops.
Look:	That's it. We'll put the three sculptures back here, Zhang Fei, Liu Bei and Guan Yu. All life-sized and in exactly the same positions.
Seeland:	Look…
Look:	Freeze!
Seeland:	…
Look:	Where you stand is also important. Let me mark it down.
	Eu Look takes out a pen. He draws a circle around New Seeland.

歐陸：　　劉關張！

　　　　　【靜默片刻】

辛西蘭：　你再講一遍。

歐陸：　　踏破鐵鞋無覓處⋯⋯

辛西蘭：　得來全靠 ―

歐陸：　　劉關張。

　　　　　【靜默片刻】

辛西蘭：　哈哈。

歐陸：　　你終於也笑得出了。

辛西蘭：　哈哈哈⋯⋯

歐陸：　　停。

辛西蘭：　⋯⋯

歐陸：　　稍過去一點，讓個位置出來。

　　　　　【辛西蘭移動】

歐陸：　　Good ！

　　　　　【辛西蘭停止移動】

歐陸：　　就是這個位置，擺三個雕塑在這，張飛、劉備、關羽，
　　　　　每個都要實物原大，照之前的樣子擺，一模一樣。

辛西蘭：　阿 Look －

歐陸：　　不要動！

辛西蘭：　⋯⋯

歐陸：　　你這個位置也相當重要，等我畫起來。

　　　　　【歐陸拿出筆，在辛西蘭的腳下畫了一圈】

Look:	We shall worship them everyday. And you, you have to stand in exactly same place. Unbiased, Yin and Yang, you open and me closed, which simulates the relationship between heaven and earth…
Seeland:	Now I…
Look:	Now I can see the words "heaven and earth".
Seeland:	I want to say…
Look:	I built like everybody else. But why couldn't I build a hegemony?
Seeland:	…
Look:	Today I understand. It was the Yin force. We were trapped inside the Yin force for thousands of years. We took cymbals and bells with us everyday. Like Falun Gong practitioners, they are always in the corner, never the centre.
Seeland:	…
Look:	Today I understand. Only once we rid ourselves of the Yin force, can my humble paper model shop blossom into a kingdom. It can be based in little Hong Kong and extend out into the mainland. Wherever there are dead people, there will be a branch of my shop. While all the real estate developers are building luxurious apartments, I will be building new houses for the dead. I will name the houses "Wealthy Mansion", "Harbourside", "Silver Lake", "Cape Town". Isn't that a fantastic idea?
Seeland:	…
Look:	(I am talking about…)
Seeland:	(I am talking about…)
	Pause.
Seeland	Relationship.
	Pause.
Seeland	Can I move now?

歐陸： 以後每天我們都會拜一拜，而你，每次都要在這個位置，
　　　 不偏不倚、一陰一陽、你開我合，形成天下大勢……

辛西蘭： 我現在 －

歐陸： 我現在見到的，是天下兩個字。

辛西蘭： 我想跟你説……

歐陸： 別人蓋樓我也是蓋樓，為什麼我不可以像他們那樣，
　　　 蓋一個霸權出來？

辛西蘭： ……

歐陸： 我今天終於明白，原來是陰氣，我們被陰氣籠罩了幾
　　　 千年，搞得日日夜夜都要帶着這些道具像伙做人，愈
　　　 做愈像法輪功，永遠都縮在角落裏，永遠都發不了功。

辛西蘭： ……

歐陸： 我今天終於明白，只要迫走這些陰氣，我歐陸紙紮就
　　　 可以大展拳腳，很快就會變成一個王國，立足小香港，
　　　 北上大中華，只要有中國人死的地方就有我歐陸紙紮，
　　　 當所有的地產商都幫人起豪宅的時候，我就替那些死
　　　 人紮新屋，間間都是「富甲天下」、「君臨維港」、「銀
　　　 湖天峰」、「海角一號」，牛不牛逼？

辛西蘭： ……

歐陸： （我現在跟你説的是……）

辛西蘭： （我現在跟你説的是……）

　　　 【靜默片刻】

辛西蘭： 關係。

　　　 【靜默片刻】

辛西蘭： 我可以動了沒啊？

第十五場

Scene 15

Scene 15

5 minutes after Scene 13.

Keung, Ken and Goldy gather in the corridor. They are still wearing the costumes: Liu, Guan and Zhang. Keung is drinking water. Ken is eating out of a lunch box. Goldy takes out some cigarettes.

Ken   Smoking is prohibited in this area.

Goldy   What are you afraid of?

Ken   It doesn't matter. What matters is that smoking is prohibited in this area.

Goldy   Is this your problem?

Ken   It doesn't matter. What matters is that smoking is prohibited in this area.

Goldy   Just say it. No problem. Just say it's your problem and I will damn well quit.

Ken   We are at war. It's important to be disciplined.

Goldy   What are you talking about?

Ken   Air flows. If you smoke here, anyone inside will smell it within three seconds. They will do two things. First, they will question the room's ventilation. Second, they will comment that the air quality is terrible. Then they will reduce the flat's rating. More seriously, they might even leave right away. The war that we are supposed to win will become a failure, all because of your cigarette.

Goldy   Fuck you…

               Goldy tries to light a cigarette.

Keung   Put it down.

               Pause.

178

第十五場

【時間接第 13 場完結後約五分鐘】

【阿強，Ken 和黃金聚在走廊上，仍穿着「劉關張」服裝。阿強喝水，Ken 吃盒飯，黃金拿出香煙】

Ken： 這裏不能抽煙的。

黃金： 你怕什麼啊？

Ken： 我怕什麼不重要，重要的是，這裏不能抽煙。

黃金： 是不是你的問題啊？

Ken： 是不是我的問題不重要，重要的是，這裏不能抽煙。

黃金： 是你的就說是，不要緊，你他媽就說是，你說是我馬上不雞巴抽。

Ken： 現在在我們正在打一場仗，紀律非常重要。

黃金： 你他媽說什麼啊？

Ken： 空氣是流動的，你在這裏抽煙，裏面的人三秒之後就會聞到，之後，他們會有兩個反應：第一，這個單位的隔煙效果好差；第二，這裏空氣質素惡劣，然後，他們會馬上降低這個單位評價，更嚴重的是，馬上走人。於是，原本可以打得贏的一場仗，就因為你一支煙，而燒得一敗塗地。

黃金： 去你二姐夫……

【黃金拿出打火機欲點煙】

阿強： 放下。

【靜默片刻】

Keung takes away the lighter.

Goldy throws away the cigarette in his hand.

Ken   Littering is prohibited here.

Pause.

Goldy   OK.

Goldy picks up the cigarette.

Goldy   Consider the greater good.

Pause.

Goldy   Sacrifice myself for a greater good? I can do it.

Pause.

Goldy   I can fucking do anything. OK?

Ken   You can't.

Goldy   …

Ken   You are not in character.

Goldy   …

Ken   Keung is different.

Keung   …

Ken   Keung is totally inside out, even when he twitched. That's why he was so convincing when he twitched. That's what I mean by "I can do it."

Goldy   …

Ken   Why can he do it and you cannot?

Goldy   …

【黃金收起打火機】

【黃金把手中的香煙掉在地上】

Ken： 這裏不可以隨便扔垃圾的。

【靜默片刻】

黃金： OK.

【黃金撿起香煙】

黃金： 以大局為重。

【靜默片刻】

黃金： 犧牲小我，完成大我，我做得到。

【靜默片刻】

黃金： 我他媽什麼都能做到，OK？

Ken： 你做不到。

黃金： ⋯⋯

Ken： 你進入不了角色。

黃金： ⋯⋯

Ken： 阿強就不同了。

阿強： ⋯⋯

Ken： 阿強整個人進去了，又再抽離出來，連筋都一起抽了，所以他抽筋抽得很有說服力，這才叫做得到。

黃金： ⋯⋯

Ken： 為什麼他做得到你做不到呢？

黃金： ⋯⋯

第十六場

Scene 16

Scene 16

Immediately after Scene 14.

Only Eu Look and New Seeland are in the flat.

Seeland: A kind of relationship.

Look: …

Seeland: A relationship between man and life.

Look: …

Seeland: The relationship between man and life is the relationship between man and house.

Look: …

Seeland: The relationship between man and house is the relationship between me and this flat.

Look: …

Seeland: The relationship between me and this flat is the relationship between you and this flat.

Look: …

Seeland: The relationship between you and this flat is ultimately the relationship between you and me.

Look: …

Seeland: You and me.

Look: …

Seeland: You and me.

Look: …

Seeland: It's that simple.

Look: …

Seeland: I have been thinking, it really is that simple.

第十六場

【時間緊接第 14 場結束】

【單位內只有歐陸和辛西蘭】

辛西蘭： 一種關係。

歐陸： ……

辛西蘭： 一種人和住的關係。

歐陸： ……

辛西蘭： 人和住的關係就是人和屋的關係。

歐陸： ……

辛西蘭： 人和屋的關係就是我和這個單位的關係。

歐陸： ……

辛西蘭： 這個單位和我的關係也就是你和這間屋的關係。

歐陸： ……

辛西蘭： 你和這間屋的關係最後是等於我和你的關係。

歐陸： ……

辛西蘭： 我和你。

歐陸： ……

辛西蘭： You, and me.

歐陸： ……

辛西蘭： 就是這麼簡單。

歐陸： ……

辛西蘭： 我一直都以為是這麼簡單。

Look: How complicated can it be?

Seeland: It was only me and you ten years ago…

Look: There's still only me and you today…

Seeland: But I never knew there was a kingdom between me and you.

Look: It hasn't been built yet.

Seeland: But it has been there.

Look: It's only imaginary.

Seeland: But it has been affecting me for the past ten years!

Look: …

Seeland: If we hadn't met those three suspect sculptures, how many more decades would we have had to wait?

Look: …

Seeland: How many more decades do I have?

Look: …

Seeland: Waiting is not a problem.

Look: …

Seeland: The problem is…

Look: It can be resolved.

Seeland: Did you know what I was thinking?

Look: Relationship.

Seeland: …

Look: Our relationship is built on piled foundations.

Seeland: …

Look: It never shakes.

歐陸：　　有多複雜呢？

辛西蘭：　十年前只有我和你……

歐陸：　　今天也都只是我和你……

辛西蘭：　但是我從來都不知道，原來我和你之間，還有一座王國。

歐陸：　　它還沒出現。

辛西蘭：　它早就存在。

歐陸：　　它只是一個想像。

辛西蘭：　它影響了我十年啊！

歐陸：　　……

辛西蘭：　如果今天不是遇到三個疑似人類的雕塑，我還要等多少個十年啊？

歐陸：　　……

辛西蘭：　我還有多少個十年啊？

歐陸：　　……

辛西蘭：　等不是問題。

歐陸：　　……

辛西蘭：　問題是……

歐陸：　　可以解決。

辛西蘭：　你知道我在想什麼嗎？

歐陸：　　關係。

辛西蘭：　……

歐陸：　　我們的關係，是建立在一個打完樁的地基上面。

辛西蘭：　……

歐陸：　　一直都沒動搖過。

第十七場

Scene 17

Scene 17

Immediately after Scene 15.

In the corridor.

Ken   For me, winning is not the reason to fight. Winning is just a means. The real goal is to make a better world. That way we can live a more meaningful life.

Goldy   …

Ken   But you, you just want to win this one.

Goldy   …

Ken   After this one, what will happen to the world? To you? You haven't thought of that. All you can think of is winning. You don't have any beliefs. No imagination. No insight.

Goldy   …

Ken   You are not serious. You're careless, rough, short sighted, immature.

Goldy   …

Ken   I regret ever working with someone like you.

Goldy   (You)…

Ken   (You)…

Pause.

Ken   Don't answer me.

Goldy   …

Ken   This is a question to myself. This is my own problem. It has nothing to do with you. I am not talking to you. I am only asking myself. Why do I work with someone like you?

Goldy   (I)…

第十七場

【時間接第 15 場完結時】

【走廊】

Ken： 對我來說，打仗的目的，不是要贏。贏，只不過是一種手段，真正的目的，是要令這個世界更加美好，人類生活得更有意義。

黃金： ⋯⋯

Ken： 但是你，你只想贏一局。

黃金： ⋯⋯

Ken： 一局之後，這個世界會怎樣呢？你自己又會怎樣呢？你完全沒想過，你除了想贏一局之外你什麼都沒想過 ─ 你沒信念、沒想像、沒 Insight。

黃金： ⋯⋯

Ken： 你這就叫做隨便、庸俗、粗糙、目光短淺、低層次。

黃金： ⋯⋯

Ken： 我很後悔，為什麼我會跟一個這樣的人合作呢？

黃金： （你）─

Ken： （你）─

【靜默片刻】

Ken： 不要回答我。

黃金： ⋯⋯

Ken： 我只是問自己，是我自己的問題，不關你事，我現在不是說你，我只是質疑我自己，為什麼我會跟一個這樣的人合作呢？

黃金： （我）─

Ken	(I)…
Ken	I have to be responsible to myself.
Goldy	…
Ken	I wish you would all support my suggestions.
Goldy	…
Ken	I suggest we change our shares from three three four to four four two.

Pause.

Ken	What do you think?
Goldy	Who takes the two?
Ken	I am asking your opinion.
Goldy	Me?
Ken	If you have an opinion, let me hear it.

Pause.

Goldy	Keung, is this how you work?
Ken	It doesn't matter how Keung works.
Goldy	I didn't utter a damn word when you suggested three three four.
Ken	What matters is your opinion.
Goldy	You mother fucker you want me to only take two?
Ken	Just say it.
Goldy	You are fucking castrating me!
Ken	Don't waste our time.

Pause.

Goldy	Say it. Who takes two?

Ken： （我）一

Ken： 要對我自己負責。

黃金： ……

Ken： 我希望大家接受我的建議。

黃金： ……

Ken： 我想將三三四改為四四二。

【靜默片刻】

Ken： 你們有沒有意見？

黃金： 誰拿二？

Ken： 我是問你們的意見。

黃金： 我嗎？

Ken： 有意見就說出來。

【靜默片刻】

黃金： 阿強，你是不是這麼幹？

Ken： 阿強怎麼幹不重要。

黃金： 之前三三四我他媽都沒計較了。

Ken： 重要的是你自己的意見。

黃金： 我日你奶媽現在你居然要我拿二？

Ken： 你說就行了。

黃金： 媽逼你是想跟他一起把我給閹了。

Ken： 不要浪費時間。

【靜默片刻】

黃金： 那你說啊，誰他媽拿二啊現在？

A sound signifying Ken has received a text message on his phone.

Ken checks the message.

Goldy   *(To Keung)* You, say it, are you going to be the one that takes two?

Keung   We still don't know if we can make the deal. Why are you complaining now?

Goldy   When would be a better time for me to complain then? Should I wait until you castrate me and turn me into a eunuch, then ask where my balls are? Yeah? Who do you think I am?

Ken   Our partner.

Goldy   What?

Ken   Collaborator.

Goldy   You fucking asshole…

Ken   Mr Eu just texted me.

Goldy
/Keung: …

Ken   He asked me, that is us, to go in, in five minutes.

         Pause.

Ken   With the contract.

         Pause.

Ken   I'll ask once more. Four, four, two, any objections?

【Ken 的電話發出收到短訊的聲音】

【Ken 查看短訊】

黃金：　（對阿強）你，你說，是不是你拿二？

阿強：　現在這張單能不能結都不知道，你他媽吵雞巴吵？

黃金：　我他媽現在不吵什麼時候吵？等你們把我閹了，成了
雞巴鳥太監，然後才問：咦，我的寶貝去他媽哪了啊？
是不是啊？你他媽當我是什麼啊？

Ken：　Partner.

黃金：　什麼？

Ken：　合作伙伴。

黃金：　你個屄毛……

Ken：　歐先生剛剛 Send 了條短訊給我。

黃金
/ 阿強：　……

Ken：　他叫我，也就是我們，五分鐘之後進去。

【靜默片刻】

Ken：　帶着合約。

【靜默片刻】

Ken：　我再問一次，四四二，有沒有人反對？

第十八場
Scene 18

Scene 18

5 minutes after Scene 16.

Eu Look and New Seeland are in the show flat. They are both holding mobile phones.

Eu Look has just sent a message and puts away his mobile phone.

New Seeland presses a couple of buttons on her mobile phone, then also puts it away.

Look: It's done.

Seeland: Me too.

They toast.

Look: As I said, no problem.

Seeland: I can't see any problems.

Look: I said, no problem.

Seeland: It's resolved, no problem.

Look: I asked them to come in, in five minutes.

Seeland: Five minutes?

Look: Or now?

Seeland: Do we have enough?

Look: Money?

Seeland: I've never worried about money.

Look: That's right.

Seeland: What's right?

Look: What?

Seeland: You think I'm worried about money?

第十八場

【距第 16 場結束約五分鐘】

【單位內，只有歐陸和辛西蘭，兩人各拿着手機】

【歐陸用手機寄出了一個短訊，放下手機】

【辛西蘭在她的手機上按了幾下，亦放下手機】

歐陸：　　搞定。

辛西蘭：　我也搞定。

【兩人碰杯飲酒】

歐陸：　　我都説沒問題了。

辛西蘭：　我也相信問題不大。

歐陸：　　我是説沒問題啊。

辛西蘭：　解決了就沒了嘛。

歐陸：　　我叫他們五分鐘之後進來。

辛西蘭：　五分鐘？

歐陸：　　可以馬上的喔。

辛西蘭：　夠嗎？

歐陸：　　錢？

辛西蘭：　我從來都沒擔心過錢。

歐陸：　　那不就是囉。

辛西蘭：　是什麼啊？

歐陸：　　吓？

辛西蘭：　你以為我擔心錢？

Look: I know you aren't.

Seeland: Why did you ask "what" just now?

Look: …

Seeland: Obviously, you don't know what I am talking about.

Look: You are talking about our relationship.

Seeland: I've been talking about it this whole time but you still don't know what I am saying.

Look: You are talking about our relationship.

Seeland: Why did you mention money just now?

Look: I thought you were worried about money.

            Pause.

            New Seeland takes the mobile phone on the table and press a button on it. A recording of their conversation can be heard…

Seeland: You think I am worried about money?

Look: I know you aren't.

            New Seeland presses the phone again. Another excerpt of their conversation can be heard...

Seeland: Why did you mention money just now?

Look: I thought you were worried about money.

            New Seeland presses the phone and repeats the broadcast.

Seeland: You said you knew I don't worry about money. Then you said you thought I was worried about money. These two sentences are contradictory. There are ten seconds in between them. That means, in the space of ten seconds, you completely reversed your perspective. What you have thrown over is not a table nor a chair, but a human being. It's me. The one who has lived with you in the paper model shop for ten years.

歐陸：　　我知道你不是。

辛西蘭：　那你剛剛「吓」什麼？

歐陸：　　……

辛西蘭：　好明顯你不知道我説什麼。

歐陸：　　你説的是關係嘛。

辛西蘭：　我説了這麼久你都不知道我説什麼。

歐陸：　　你説的是我和你的關係嘛。

辛西蘭：　那你剛剛又説錢？

歐陸：　　我以為你擔心錢嘛。

　　　　　【靜默片刻】

　　　　　【辛西蘭拿起枱上的手機，按了幾下，播出剛才兩人對話的一個片段】

辛西蘭：　你以為我擔心錢？

歐陸：　　我知道你不是。

　　　　　【辛西蘭再按手機，又播出另一個片段】

辛西蘭：　那你剛剛又説錢？

歐陸：　　我以為你擔心錢嘛。

　　　　　【辛西蘭按停手機，再按幾下，重播以上兩段對話】

辛西蘭：　你説你知道我不是擔心錢，然後你又説你以為我擔心錢，這兩句話一正一負，互相矛盾，中間隔了十秒，也就是説，在十秒之內，你可以推翻你之前説過的話。而被你推翻的，不是一張枱、不是一張樽，而是一個人 — 是我，一個和你一起，在一間紙紮舖生活了十年的，我。

Look:	When did this flat turn into a court?
Seeland:	This is not a court. This is a home, or, a prospective home. We spend so much time focusing on living in a home. But I also care about living.
Look:	…
Seeland:	Are you sure we will make it in this flat for the next thirty years?
Look:	…
Seeland:	This is not only a problem. This is a big problem.
Look:	…
Seeland:	We only have five minutes, what can we resolve?
Look:	Why did you record our conversation?
Seeland:	Didn't you see?
Look:	…
Seeland:	I did it right in front of you. You didn't see?
Look:	…
Seeland:	What did you see then?
Look:	…
Seeland:	Heaven and earth?
Look:	…
Seeland:	Your heaven and earth.
Look:	…
Seeland:	It seems to me there isn't any place for me in your heaven and earth.
	Pause.
Look:	I want to ask a question.

歐陸： 這裏什麼時候變成法庭了？

辛西蘭： 這裏不是法庭，這裏是一間屋子，或者，是一個疑似屋子，屋子講的是生活，我關心的，都是生活。

歐陸： ……

辛西蘭： 你認為未來 30 年，我們真可以在這個單位裏面，一起生活？

歐陸： ……

辛西蘭： 這個不僅是一個問題，而且還是一個好大的問題。

歐陸： ……

辛西蘭： 五分鐘，可以解決嗎？

歐陸： 為什麼你要錄音啊？

辛西蘭： 你之前沒見到嗎？

歐陸： ……

辛西蘭： 我在你面前做的事，你完全沒見到？

歐陸： ……

辛西蘭： 那你見到什麼啊？

歐陸： ……

辛西蘭： 天下。

歐陸： ……

辛西蘭： 你的天下。

歐陸： ……

辛西蘭： 你的天下裏面，似乎沒包括我。

【靜默片刻】

歐陸： 我想問一個問題。

Seeland:	This is not a court.
Look:	Why did you record our conversation?
Seeland:	I was afraid I would get it wrong.
Look:	…
Seeland:	Since you started talking about mortuaries today, you've talked about the concept of living and the meaning of life. Then you mentioned Yin and Yang, together with Zhang Fei, Liu Bei and Guan Yu. I don't quite understand all this. Then you talked about your kingdom, our relationship. You said our relationship is established on a piled foundation. Then… I'm beginning to understand…
Look:	…
Seeland:	Your basis, is the foundation for your kingdom, a paper kingdom.
Look:	…
Seeland:	What has that got to do with me?
Look:	…
Seeland:	I'm afraid I've got it all wrong.
Look:	…

Ken enters, Keung and Goldy follow. They are in costume: Liu, Guan and Zhang, like guards of honour.

Keung holds a fabulous folder with a document inside "Provisional Agreement for Sale & Purchase".

Goldy is holding a fabulous set of pens in a pen holder.

Pause.

辛西蘭： 這裏不是法庭。

歐陸： 為什麼你要錄音啊？

辛西蘭： 我怕我聽錯。

歐陸： ……

辛西蘭： 今天從你說停屍房開始，一路說到住的概念，住的含義，然後說到陰氣、陽氣，然後說到張飛、劉備、關羽……所有這些我都不是很明白，然後你又說到你的王國，然後你又說我們的關係。我們的關係，是建立在一個打完樁的地基上面，然後……我慢慢明白……

歐陸： ……

辛西蘭： 你的地基，似乎只是要建立你的王國，一個紙紮王國。

歐陸： ……

辛西蘭： 這些跟我有什麼關係呢？

歐陸： ……

辛西蘭： 我開始懷疑我的理解能力。

歐陸： ……

辛西蘭： 我怕我聽錯。

歐陸： ……

【Ken 領着阿強和黃金入，三人仍穿着「劉關張」的服裝，像一儀仗隊】

【阿強捧着一個華麗的文件套（Folder），套上有一份文件（樓宇買賣臨時合約）】

【黃金捧着一對華麗的筆座，筆座上插着華麗的筆】

【靜默片刻】

205

Seeland: I feel like going bowling.

             New Seeland tries to exit.

Look: Why don't you try playing golf?

             New Seeland stops.

辛西蘭：　我想下去試試那個保齡球場。

　　　　　【辛西蘭欲下】

歐陸：　　不如試一下打 Golf 吧。

　　　　　【辛西蘭停】

第十九場

Scene 19

Scene 19

10 minutes after the previous scene.

Keung, Ken and Goldy are sitting around a table in the show flat.

There is a folder and a pen-holder on the table and an astro turf putting green on the floor. There are some golf balls on the carpet.

Eu Look is holding a golf club, putting the golf balls.

New Seeland stands or sits.

Look: When it comes to living, I am truly persistent.

Seeland: Everybody has their own drive.

Look: I started visiting show flats as a teenager. Once I started, I was hooked.

Seeland: Even haunted flats.

Look: Every time I visited a show flat, I left fulfilled.

Seeland: It's like a hunger.

Look: You are full for a while after visiting, but you are soon hungry again.

Seeland: Especially after visiting show flats.

Look: What do show flats show?

Seeland: …

Look: I know that well.

Seeland: …

Look: In the past, the paper models people burned household goods for their ancestors. Nowadays, everyone orders an additional item. A mansion.

第十九場

【距上場約 10 分鐘】

【單位內，阿強、Ken 和黃金圍枴而坐】

【枴上放着文件套和筆座】

【地上舖了一張綠草地毯，毯上放了一些高爾夫球】

【歐陸拿着一支高爾夫球桿，推球或打球】

【辛西蘭在地上野餐】

歐陸：　　關於「住」這個問題，我的確是很執着。

辛西蘭：　每個人都會有些堅持。

歐陸：　　十幾歲開始學人家看房子，一看就上癮。

辛西蘭：　連凶宅都不放過。

歐陸：　　每次看完一個單位，都有一種滿足感。

辛西蘭：　好像飢餓。

歐陸：　　看完就飽了一點，但是很快又會餓。

辛西蘭：　尤其是看示範單位。

歐陸：　　示範單位其實示範什麼呢？

辛西蘭：　⋯⋯

歐陸：　　我很清楚。

辛西蘭：　⋯⋯

歐陸：　　以前的人燒衣紙，主要都是生活用品，但是現在大家都會多一個要求，就是豪宅。

Pause.

Look: Prior to making a paper model house, I always make a show flat for my client. Deceased people need to be made up before they are placed in the coffin, so do show flats. They need makeup before being shown to people. That is the problem. Every time I walk into a show flat, I feel like I'm walking into a mortuary. Every time, until today...

Seeland: Have you visited the pool today?

Eu Look doesn't answer.

Seeland: I looked down at the pool from the roof just now. The shape of it seemed familiar. As if I'd seen it before. I googled it on my phone and ha, I knew it.

Pause.

Seeland: It's High Island Reservoir.

Pause.

Seeland: Does anyone know who designs the swimming pools for houses?

No one answers.

Seeland: Feng Shui masters.

Pause.

Seeland: I don't have any beliefs. But I am willing to accept that Gods or ghosts exist. I am also ready to believe that putting a pool like High Island Reservoir down there among the buildings will encourage a prosperous future and a good fortune for all the tenants. But the reason I buy a flat is not for a prosperous future or good fortune. (The reason I buy a flat is...)

Look: (The reason I buy a flat is...)

Pause.

【靜默片刻】

歐陸： 每做一棟房子之前，我都會先紮一個示範單位給客戶看一下，死人要化妝才能入殮，示範單位也是一樣，要經過化妝才可以打開門給人看，問題就在這裏，每次當我走進一個示範單位，我都覺得好像走進一間殮房，直到今天……

辛西蘭： 你參觀了游泳池沒？

【歐陸沒有回應】

辛西蘭： 我之前在天台看下去，覺得這個游泳池的形狀好面熟，好像在哪裏見過。我用手機上網一 Check，哈，原來真是。

【靜默片刻】

辛西蘭： 是萬宜水庫。

【靜默片刻】

辛西蘭： 現在的住宅游泳池是什麼人設計的，你們知不知道啊？

【沒有人回應】

辛西蘭： 是風水師傅。

【靜默片刻】

辛西蘭： 我沒有宗教信仰，但我願意相信，這個世界真的有神、有鬼，我甚至願意相信，擺一個好像萬宜水庫這樣的游泳池在樓下，可以讓整棟房子的人風生水起，大富大貴。但是我買樓，絕對不是因為我要風生水起，大富大貴。（我買樓，是因為我要……）

歐陸： （我買樓，是因為我要……）

【靜默片刻】

Look: to serve the dead.

            Pause.

Look: (*To Ken, Keung and Goldy*) If you don't own a luxurious
            house when you are alive, you can get one after you've died.
            Alive, Chris Patten, Tung Chee-hwa and Donald Tsang
            couldn't help you. CY Leung and Henry Tang couldn't
            either. But it doesn't matter. My paper model shop can
            definitely help you. I am a real creator!

Seeland: No.

            Pause.

Seeland: I think you've made a mistake.

            Pause.

Seeland: You are not a creator. You are a designer.

            Pause.

Look: I don't understand. Why can't you appreciate me more?

Seeland: There is only one man who creates. Rather he is not a man,
            he is God. God created the world and we design the rest.

Look: OK. Every inch of this space you see was designed by man.
            So what? What's the problem with it?

Seeland: The problem is "if".

            Pause.

Seeland: If for the next thirty years, we have to live in a fully designed
            space. How will it be?

            Pause.

Seeland: What I mean is, a designed life and relationship.

            Pause.

歐陸： 我要為死人服務。

【靜默片刻】

歐陸： （對 Ken、阿強和黃金）你們在生的時候沒豪宅，死了之後就會有，彭定康幫不到你、董建華幫不到你、曾蔭權幫不到你、梁振英唐英年都未必能幫到你！但不要緊，我歐陸紙紮一定可以幫到你。我，是一個真真正正的創造者！

辛西蘭： No.

【靜默片刻】

辛西蘭： 我想你搞錯了。

【靜默片刻】

辛西蘭： 你做的不是創作，是設計。

【靜默片刻】

歐陸： 我不明白，為什麼你不能以一個欣賞的角度來看我。

辛西蘭： 全世界只有一個人搞創作，嚴格來講他不是人 ── 是神、是上帝。上帝創造完這個世界之後，所有人搞的都不是創作，是設計。

歐陸： OK，現在你所見到的一切，這裏每一寸空間，全部都是由人設計出來的，那又怎樣？有什麼問題呢？

辛西蘭： 問題是如果。

【靜默片刻】

辛西蘭： 如果未來 30 年，我都要生活在一種「設計」裏面，將會是怎麼一回事？

【靜默片刻】

辛西蘭： 我的意思是，一種「設計」出來的生活和關係。

【靜默片刻】

Seeland: Ten years ago you brought me to the foundation site. It was soundly designed. I liked it and appreciated it. But ten years later, I realise I am just a pile, a pillar in this flat, or a wall, a scene, an element for design. I can't take it.

Pause.

Seeland: I think I'd rather go bowling.

Seeland exits.

Look: *(To Ken, Keung and Goldy)* Have you been at war?

A watermelon rolls in.

Eu Look breaks it with a golf club.

辛西蘭： 十年前你帶我去工地看人打樁，是一種設計，我很喜歡，我很欣賞；但是十年後的今天，我發覺原來我只不過是一支樁，是這個單位的一條柱，或者是一堵牆、一個背景、一個被人設計的元素，我受不了。

【靜默片刻】

辛西蘭： 我想我還是喜歡打保齡球多一點。

【辛西蘭下】

歐陸： （對 Ken，黃金及阿強）你們打過仗沒有？

【一個西瓜滾了進來】

【歐陸用高爾夫球桿將西瓜打爆】

第二十場
Scene 20

Scene 20

Five seconds after the previous scene.

Goldy, Ken and Keung are in the show flat. They are in the same position as in the previous scene. They are frozen.

Suddenly they all unfreeze together.

Keung: Wow…

Goldy: That was fucking crazy…

Keung: My back is fucking twisted…

Goldy: What the fuck was he talking about…

Keung: Do you have to know?

Goldy: What?

Ken starts to eat the watermelon.

Keung: You don't need to know what the fuck they were talking about.

Goldy: Fuck you. I have taken courses. The teacher said we have to pay close attention to what the client says…

Keung: All you need to do is pretend. You don't need to use so many facial expressions. I was watching you frowning just now, what the fuck are you trying so hard for.

Goldy: Pardon me?

Keung: What are you fighting for.

Goldy: What am I fighting for?

Keung: The client asks you to sit, you sit. That's all you need. You don't need to show him whether you understand or not.

第二十場

【距上場約五秒】

【單位內，只有黃金、Ken 和阿強，坐姿與上場一樣，彷彿被「凝結」了】

【三人忽然同時從「凝結」中釋放出來】

阿強：　嘩……

黃金：　我日他個親娘……

阿強：　坐得我他媽屁眼兒都歪了……

黃金：　完全不知道他他媽的講什麼鳥東西，媽逼他講什麼我他媽完全他媽的不知道，你說他他媽的講的是他媽的什麼鳥東西，我他媽的什麼他媽的都不知道媽逼……

阿強：　你需要知道什麼？

黃金：　什麼？

【Ken 開始吃西瓜】

阿強：　你完全不需要知道他們講的是什麼鳥東西的。

黃金：　去你奶奶個腿，我上過 Course，老師說一定要聆聽 —— Listen，聽清楚客戶講什麼……

阿強：　裝一下就行啦，你不用給什麼鳥表情，我他媽之前看你的樣子，就這樣皺着個鳥眉頭。What the fuck are you qianging for？

黃金：　什麼？

阿強：　你他媽搶什麼啊？

黃金：　我他媽搶什麼？

阿強：　客戶叫你坐這裏，你就坐這裏囉，你坐這裏就行了，你他媽不需要讓他知道你能不能聽懂他講什麼啊。

Goldy:	I communicate with my clients? What's wrong with that?
Keung:	Who do you think you are? Why does he have to communicate with you? Do you understand why Mona Lisa smiles at you? No one knows. Why does no one know? Because no one needs to know. It's the same thing, we all sit here and listen to him. There's no need for him to know if we understand or not. Look at all your facial expressions. What are you fighting for?
Goldy:	I just want to help. OK?
Keung:	You are not helping the situation. You are ruining it.
Goldy:	What have I ruined?
Keung:	Aesthetic feeling.
Goldy:	What?
Keung:	The whole scene is destroyed. It's not aesthetically pleasant any more.
Goldy:	You're lecturing me on aesthetic feeling?
Keung:	You just don't fucking understand. I have to explain in terms of feeling. If you weren't so primitive and vulgar we could discuss aesthetics. It's more advanced.
	Pause.
Goldy:	So what?
Keung:	…
Goldy:	We don't need to eat at an advanced level?
Keung:	…
Goldy:	I need to.
Keung:	…
Goldy:	Not only do I need to eat, but I also need to eat meat. Not only do I need to eat meat, but I also need to be vulgar.

黃金：　　我跟客戶交流啊，有什麼問題啊？

阿強：　　你是他什麼人啊？他為什麼要跟你交流啊？蒙娜麗莎對着你笑，你知不知道她笑個鳥啊？沒人知道的，為什麼沒人知道啊？是因為沒人需要知道啊。同樣道理，我們坐這裏聽他説話，他是不需要知道我們能不能聽懂的。你給這麼多鳥表情，你他媽爭什麼啊？

黃金：　　我是想幫到這件事，OK？

阿強：　　你現在不是幫這件事，你是在破壞。

黃金：　　我破壞了什麼啊？

阿強：　　美感。

黃金：　　什麼？

阿強：　　整個畫面全他媽花掉了，完全沒有美感。

黃金：　　你跟我談美感？

阿強：　　我怕你他媽不明白，所以才跟你談美感，如果你他媽的不這麼庸俗，我會跟你談美學，層次他媽高很多。

【靜默片刻】

黃金：　　那又怎樣？

阿強：　　……

黃金：　　層次高是不是他媽的就不需要吃飯了？

阿強：　　……

黃金：　　我要喔。

阿強：　　……

黃金：　　我不只要吃飯，我還要吃肉，我不僅要吃肉，我他媽的還要吃得庸俗。

Keung: …

Goldy: So what?

Keung: …

Goldy: Is it a sin to be vulgar?

Keung: …

Goldy: Do I have to die for it?

Keung: …

Goldy: I am fine with it if you want me to die.

Keung: …

Goldy: To Ken You, tell me if you want me to die?

            Ken continues eating watermelon.

Goldy: Thank God you are all mute. Otherwise I don't know what I'd do.

            Ken continues eating watermelon.

Goldy: I mean, I don't know what you are going to do.

            Ken continues eating watermelon.

Goldy: I mean, without Zhang Fei, can Liu Bei and Guan Gong get a ride?

            Ken continues eating watermelon.

Goldy: Where do you want to go?

            Ken continues eating watermelon.

Goldy: I don't fucking know where you want to go you mother fucker. We agreed to fight together for an equal share. Fuck you! First you change it to three, three, four, and then all of a sudden you change it to four, four, two. You mother fucker, fine! I am fine to take less. On the condition that I can fucking go back to my homeland. But you assholes…

阿強： ……

黃金： 那又怎樣？

阿強： ……

黃金： 庸俗是不是罪來的？

阿強： ……

黃金： 用不用死啊？

阿強： ……

黃金： 如果你們要我死也可以喔。

阿強： ……

黃金： （對 Ken）你，你告訴我，你是不是想我死？

【Ken 繼續吃西瓜】

黃金： 好在你們不吭聲，否則我真不知道怎麼辦。

【Ken 繼續吃西瓜】

黃金： 我是説，我不知道「你們」怎麼辦。

【Ken 繼續吃西瓜】

黃金： 我是説，劉備關羽，媽逼少了張飛，你們上得了車？

【Ken 繼續食西瓜】

黃金： 你們想去哪？

【Ken 繼續吃西瓜】

黃金： 我真他媽不知道你們想去哪，媽逼明明説好一起上，一人一票。媽逼説着説着就他媽變成三三四，媽逼三啊三啊又他媽變四四二，OK！操他媽的四四二我都不計較，我少拿點，沒問題，只要能回故鄉我都不計較，但你們倆這屌樣……

225

Ken continues eating watermelon.

Goldy: Have you got a homeland?

Ken continues eating watermelon.

Goldy: Don't you need to go home?

Ken continues eating watermelon.

Goldy: Are you even fucking human beings?

Ken: Many a time have I dreamt of my homeland.

Goldy: Pardon me?

Ken: Forever my gravestone faces my birthplace.

Goldy: What the fuck are you talking about?

Ken: Mr Eu told me about it.

Pause.

Ken: His family name is Eu. Look is his first name. Eu Look, it
           reminds me of looking at my homeland.

Pause.

Ken: Mountains, rivers, grassland, churches, Fortresses.

Pause.

Ken: A lyrical homeland.

Pause.

Ken: But it doesn't belong to Hong Kong.

Pause.

Ken: Hong Kong is a city with no homeland.

Pause.

Ken: Have you got a homeland?

Pause.

【Ken 繼續吃西瓜】

黃金：　　你們沒故鄉嗎？

【Ken 繼續吃西瓜】

黃金：　　你們他媽不用回家嗎？

【Ken 繼續吃西瓜】

黃金：　　你們他媽還是不是人啊我操你祖宗？

Ken：　　活着夢回故土。

黃金：　　什麼？

Ken：　　死後墓向原鄉。

黃金：　　你講雞巴毛啊？

Ken：　　是歐先生跟我說的。

【靜默片刻】

Ken：　　他姓歐，叫陸，他叫歐陸，聽起來已經像一個故鄉。

【靜默片刻】

Ken：　　山脈、河流、草原、教堂、城堡。

【靜默片刻】

Ken：　　一個很抒情的故鄉。

【靜默片刻】

Ken：　　但是完全不屬於香港。

【靜默片刻】

Ken：　　香港，是一個沒有故鄉的城市。

【靜默片刻】

Ken：　　你有故鄉嗎？

【靜默片刻】

Ken: Where is it?

           Pause.

Ken: Before '97? After SARS? Before the economic crisis? Or
           After?

           Pause.

Ken: Can you go back?

           Pause.

Ken: Do you think you can go back?

           Pause.

Ken: All you can do is: Dream of your homeland where your
           gravestone faces your birthplace.

Ken: That way it will be commemorated forever.

           Pause.

           Goldy exits.

Keung: Where are you going?

           Goldy stops.

Goldy: I'm going out to tell people that this flat is an unauthorised
           building. The whole building is unauthorised. I will also
           say this flat is haunted, someone died here, the drainage
           is problematic, it is built on top of haunted land, corpses
           everywhere. Whoever I meet, I will tell them the same story.
           I will talk, talk, talk and talk until the economy declines.

Keung: You mother fucker…

Ken: I want you to know what it is to perish together.

Keung: If you have a problem let's talk about it. Getting mad
           doesn't help anything, does it?

Goldy: He wants me to die.

Ken：　你的故鄉在哪啊？

【靜默片刻】

Ken：　97 之前？沙士之後？風暴之前？還是海嘯之後啊？

【靜默片刻】

Ken：　回得去嗎？

【靜默片刻】

Ken：　你以為你回得去嗎？

【靜默片刻】

Ken：　你現在唯一可以做的就是：活着夢回故土，死後墓向原鄉。

【靜默片刻】

Ken：　也就是永遠的憑吊。

【靜默片刻】

【黃金向外走】

阿強：　你去哪啊？

【黃金停步】

黃金：　我出去跟人説，我説這個單位是違章建築，整棟樓都是違章建築。還有這間是凶宅，媽的死過人、燒過炭、爆過屎渠，這塊地皮以前是亂葬岡、屍橫遍野，我見十個人我就跟十個人説，我見一百個人我就跟一百個人説，説説説説……媽的説到黃掉為止。

阿強：　我操……

黃金：　我他媽要你們知道什麼叫玉石俱焚。

阿強：　不行講到行，你做瘋狗有鳥用？

黃金：　他想我死喔。

229

Keung: Nobody wants you to die.

Goldy: If nobody wants me to die, why does he keep lecturing me about life and death? Homeland and birthplace? What the fuck is that? What the fuck is he talking about?

Keung: You don't fucking care what he's talking about. Me neither. You don't fucking know, I haven't got a fucking clue either. I told you, you don't have to die, you have my word.

Goldy: OK.

Pause.

Goldy: Three, three, four.

Keung: What?

Goldy: If you don't want me to die it has to be three, three, four.

Keung: We've already fucking agreed on four, four, two!

Goldy: I have to get to my homeland. I need three, three, four.

Keung: No going back.

Goldy: Go back.

Keung: Four, four, two.

Goldy: Three, three, four.

Keung: Four, four, two.

Goldy: Three, three, four.

Ken: No.

Keung /Goldy: …

Ken: It should be five, four, one.

Pause.

Goldy: What?

阿強： 現在沒人想你死。

黃金： 媽逼沒人想我死，他跟我說什麼生前死後？故土原鄉？什麼玩意？他說的啥雞巴玩意？

阿強： 你他媽不用理他說什麼鳥，我他媽也不知道他說什麼鳥！You don't fucking know, I don't fucking know either! 總之我說你不用死你就不用死。

黃金： OK.

【靜默片刻】

黃金： 三三四。

阿強： 什麼？

黃金： 不想我死就三三四。

阿強： 媽的已經說好四四二了。

黃金： 我現在要回故鄉，三三四。

阿強： 媽的沒得回頭的。

黃金： 一定要往後走。

阿強： 四四二。

黃金： 三三四。

阿強： 四四二。

黃金： 三三四。

Ken： No.

阿強
/ 黃金： ⋯⋯

Ken： 是五四一。

【靜默片刻】

黃金： 什麼？

Ken: Five, four, one. Work more, earn more.

Goldy: How have you worked more?

Ken: I finished the whole watermelon and none of you helped me out.

Goldy: That has nothing to do with me! You ate the watermelon because you like watermelon!

Ken: Just because I eat watermelon doesn't mean I like watermelon.

Goldy: You finished the whole fucking watermelon but still deny the fact that you like watermelon?

Ken: I eat it, because I want to understand the meaning inside it.

           Pause.

           Goldy pushes Ken all of a sudden.

           Ken collapses.

           Goldy takes a piece of watermelon and stuffs it into Ken's mouth.

Goldy: Meaning! Meaning! Take the whole fucking meaning! Take it you asshole! Take it!

Keung: Stop!

Goldy: Five, four, one! Five, four, one!

           Keung pushes Goldy away.

Keung: Stop it!

           Pause.

Goldy: What the fuck are you afraid of?

Keung: Are you going to shove him to death?

Goldy: What the fuck are you afraid of?

Ken： 五四一，多勞多得。

黃金： 多你個蛋啊多？

Ken： 整個西瓜我一個人吃的，你們完全沒幫忙。

黃金： 你自己喜歡吃西瓜關我鳥事啊？

Ken： 我吃西瓜並不代表我喜歡吃西瓜。

黃金： 整個西瓜被你全吃完了你他媽還說你不喜歡吃？

Ken： 我吃，是因為我想知道它裏面有什麼含意。

【靜默片刻】

【黃金忽然推 Ken】

【Ken 倒下】

【黃金拿起一塊西瓜往 Ken 嘴裏塞，一邊塞一邊罵】

黃金： 含意是吧！含意是吧！我現在給你含個蛋！快雞巴給我含啊！含啊！

阿強： 停手！

黃金： 五四一是吧！五四一是吧！

【阿強拉開黃金】

阿強： 停手啊！

【靜默片刻】

黃金： 你怕個蛋啊？

阿強： 你他媽是不是想整死他啊？

黃金： 你怕個蛋啊？

233

Keung:	OK, go ahead. If you kill him, I'll pretend I didn't see anything.

Goldy hits Keung suddenly.

Keung:	I asked you to kill him. Why the fuck are you hitting me?
Goldy:	Why are you on his side?
Keung:	I am on his side?
Goldy:	I said three, three, four. But you said four, four, two.
Keung:	Four, four, two is the final decision. We've agreed on that.
Goldy:	Whether it is three, three, four or four, four, two, you still take four. No more, no less. Why are you on his side?
Keung:	I'm not.
Goldy:	If you aren't then let's go for three, three, four.
Keung:	Even if I'm fine with it, he won't agree. He's now requesting five, four, one.
Goldy:	You fucking assholes, you still deny you are not killing me?

Goldy tries to hit Keung repeatedly. Ken gets up from the floor.

Ken:	Wearing our armour, we fight hundreds of battles. If Liu Lan is not taken we can never return.

Ken continues to eat watermelon. He speaks while he eats.

Ken:	This watermelon is very sweet.

Pause.

Ken:	Sweet and juicy.

Pause.

Ken:	Not only sweet, there's another distinct flavour.

Pause.

Ken:	The unmistakable taste of the desert.

阿強： OK，你整啊你整啊，你他媽整死他，我他媽什麼都看
　　　　不到。

　　　　【黃金忽然打阿強】

阿強： 我叫你整他啊，你幹毛打我啊？

黃金： 為什麼你要幫他？

阿強： 我幫他？

黃金： 我之前說三三四，你非要說四四二。

阿強： 四四二是最後方案，媽的都説好的了。

黃金： 無論是三三四還是四四二，你都拿四，不多不少，為
　　　　毛你要幫他？

阿強： 我沒有啊。

黃金： 沒有你就三三四。

阿強： 我他媽肯他也不肯啊，現在他還要五四一呢。

黃金： 你兩個屄毛還不是合夥整我？

　　　　【黃金正要進一步打阿強，Ken 從地上爬起】

Ken： 「黃沙百戰穿金甲，不破樓蘭終不還。」

　　　　【Ken 繼續吃西瓜，一邊吃一邊説 ─】

Ken： 這個西瓜真的好甜。

　　　　【靜默片刻】

Ken： 又甜，又多汁。

　　　　【靜默片刻】

Ken： 不單止甜，還有一種味道。

　　　　【靜默片刻】

Ken： 一種沙漠的味道。

Pause.

Ken: I wonder if this is in fact not a watermelon, but a melon.

Pause.

Ken: It grew in the desert.

Pause.

Ken: Wearing our armour, we fight hundreds of battles. If Liu Lan is not taken we can never return.

Goldy: What the fuck do you mean?

Ken: Liu Lan is a city in the desert. Until we invade it, we can never return home.

Pause.

Goldy: *(To Keung)* This is the meaning you found inside the watermelon?

Keung: What do you think?

Goldy: I think I fucking want to kill him.

Keung: I also fucking want to kill you.

Ken: When you see the Buddha, kill him.

Each of them takes out a pistol. Goldy points at Ken. Keung points at Goldy, Ken points at Keung.

A gunshot is heard.

Time flies by like a torrent.

【靜默片刻】

Ken： 我懷疑這不是西瓜，是哈密瓜。

【靜默片刻】

Ken： 它的原產地，是一片大漠。

【靜默片刻】

Ken： 「黃沙百戰穿金甲，不破樓蘭終不還。」

黃金： 什麼鳥意思啊？

Ken： 樓蘭是大漠裏面的一個城池，沒攻陷這個城池，就不可以回家。

【靜默片刻】

黃金： （對阿強）這就是西瓜的含意？

阿強： 你認為呢？

黃金： 我很想宰了他。

阿強： 我也很想宰了你。

Ken： 殺佛，是為了見佛。

【三人拔槍 ── 黃金指着 Ken、阿強指着金、Ken 指着阿強】

【槍聲響】

【時間像一條激流，隨着槍聲而去】

第二十一場

Scene 21

Scene 21

Immediately after the previous scene. But it seems that thirty years have passed.

Ken, Keung and Goldy remain the in same position as in the previous scene. Their pistols have disappeared.

Eu Look and New Seeland are in the show flat frozen.

Eu Look and New Seeland stare at Ken, Keung and Goldy. Time is frozen at a point in history.

After a moment, New Seeland and Eu Look are unfrozen – From this point on, they move and speak as if they are much older.

Look: They are still here.

Seeland: They are here everyday.

Look: They didn't even move.

Seeland: Always and forever.

Look: Spirits live forever.

Seeland: Let me pay them my respects.

           Seeland picks up some incense.

Look: Seeland…

Seeland: Yes?

Look: How much incense have you got?

           Seeland takes out three incense sticks.

Seeland: Only three.

Look: Take them.

Seeland: You can have them.

第二十一場

【距上場約一秒，但時間彷彿已過了 30 年】

【Ken，阿強和黃金保持上場完結時的姿勢，只是手中的槍不再存在】

【歐陸與辛西蘭也在單位內】

【歐與辛凝望 Ken、阿強和黃金，時間彷彿凝結在歷史的一點上】

【過了一會，辛西蘭和歐陸彷彿從凝結的時間中釋放出來 ─ 由現在開始，他們的動作節奏和說話語氣都漸見蒼老】

歐陸：　　還在這兒。

辛西蘭：　他們天天都在這。

歐陸：　　寸步不離。

辛西蘭：　天長地久。

歐陸：　　浩氣長存。

辛西蘭：　先讓我拜一拜。

　　　　　【辛西蘭取香】

歐陸：　　「晒冷」……

辛西蘭：　幹嘛？

歐陸：　　你有沒有多支香啊？

　　　　　【辛西蘭拿出三支香】

辛西蘭：　只有三支。

歐陸：　　那你自己用吧。

辛西蘭：　不如你用吧。

Look:	But you won't have any.
Seeland:	I am fine.
Look:	I am fine too.
	Pause.
Seeland:	Let me put them away.
	Pause.
Goldy:	Excuse me…
	Eu Look and New Seeland fall into deep thought.
Goldy:	Are you going to pay your respects?
	Eu Look and New Seeland remain in deep thought.
Goldy:	It's not that I don't want to persist, but I am really tired…
	Keung starts to move.
Ken:	What are you doing?
Keung:	I twitched.
Goldy:	Again?
Ken:	Stop him.
	Goldy holds Keung while Ken talks to Eu Look and New Seeland.
Ken:	Mr and Mrs Eu, time has flown by so fast. Today we have experienced a lot together in this show flat. It was an extremely fruitful experience but there is still one thing that we need to accomplish together…
	Keung screams out loud.
Goldy:	Done.
Ken:	Go back to your place.

歐陸：　　我用了你不就沒了。

辛西蘭：　我沒有也可以。

歐陸：　　你可以，我也可以。

　　　　　【靜默片刻】

辛西蘭：　那我收回去了。

　　　　　【靜默片刻】

黃金：　　兩位……

　　　　　【歐陸和辛西蘭彷彿陷入了沉思中】

黃金：　　你們還拜不拜啊？

　　　　　【歐陸與辛西蘭繼續沉思】

黃金：　　我不是不想堅持，但我真的好累……

　　　　　【阿強的身體有點異動】

Ken：　　你幹嘛啊？

阿強：　　抽筋。

黃金：　　又來？

Ken：　　停止他。

　　　　　【黃金「停止」阿強抽筋；其間，Ken 對歐陸和辛西蘭
　　　　　說話 —】

Ken：　　兩位，時間過得好快，今天，在這裏，我們一起經歷
　　　　　了好多事，真的可以稱得上是，豐盛人生。但是，還
　　　　　有一件事，一件需要我們大家一起合力完成的事……

　　　　　【阿強慘叫一聲】

黃金：　　搞定。

Ken：　　各就各位！

Ken holds a tray with the contract on it. Goldy pulls Keung to Eu Look and New Seeland and bends him over like a table. Ken puts the tray on Keung's back. Goldy takes out two golden pens in a pen holder and puts them on the tray, it is as if two country leaders are signing a treaty.

Ken: There are 15 minutes left. In 15 minutes time, "Delta Agent Group presents Trial Residency" starring Ken, Goldy and Keung will come to an end. At this critical time you must revisit the unremarkable living experience of the past hour and forty five minutes.

And together make a wise and conclusive decision.

Pause.

Ken gives a signal.

Goldy: Investing in properties is investing in happiness. If you don't have it now, you will have it in the future. If no one's ever told you that, I am telling you now. You have to believe, to make an investment, you have to find someone you can trust, an investment tool that you can rely on. You have to trust us when investing in a property. We are specialists, professionals. Trust us, we have your best interests at heart, you will receive golden treatment from Ken, Goldy and Keung Delta Agent Group.

Pause.

Ken makes another signal.

Keung: Men have personalities and so do flats. Men and flats have to "click" with each other. If not, don't take it even if it is free. Ken, Goldy and Keung Delta are practical. It has to be solid. When you walked in just now, "click," I heard that clearly. Very solid. This flat and you are meant for each other. You have "clicked."

Pause.

【Ken 拿起合約（用一個托盤盛載着），黃金把阿強拖至歐陸和辛西蘭面前，背朝天伏在地上。Ken 把托盤放在阿強背上，黃金拿出兩支插座式金筆，放在盤上（像兩國元首簽署協議書的格調）】

Ken： 還有 15 分鐘。15 分鐘之後，我們「Ken·金·強」三角連線代理集團特別呈獻的試住時間 — Trial Residency — 即將隆重結束。在這個關鍵時刻，我們相信兩位一定在重溫過去這 1 小時 45 分鐘刻骨銘心的生活體驗，然後，會作出一個英明的抉擇。

【靜默片刻】

【Ken 做了一個手勢】

黃金： 投資物業，就是投資幸福。你們現在沒有，但將來會有，如果沒人告訴你們，我現在告訴你們，你們要堅信 — 投資，一定要找最信賴的人，和最可靠的投資工具。投資物業，一定要信我們 — 專家、專業。信我們，你們將來都會有，「Ken·金·強」三角連線，盛世藏金。

【靜默片刻】

【Ken 再做一個手勢】

阿強： 人有人格，屋有屋格。人格和屋格一定要合，不合的話送給你都不要，我們「Ken·金·強」做事就這麼實在，一定要實，你們剛才一走進來，啪一聲，我聽得好清楚、好清脆，整套房跟你們，完全合拍，杠杠的！

【靜默片刻】

Kn/G/Kg: We in the real estate industry only have one desire. That is to help every client achieve their life goal. Moving from a small flat to a large one, from the lower level to the higher ones, from living in a dark box to having beautiful scenery, from street views to mountain views, from mountain views to sea views, from sea views to boundless sea views. We will be with our clients every step of the way, heart to heart, striving to match our clients… friend's greatest expectations towards the ultimate goal, to mould the world in order to improve our lives.

Pause.

From this point on, it is obvious that the gestures and speech of Eu Look and New Seeland have aged.

Look: Thirty years.

Seeland: Thirty years have passed like a day.

Look: Nothing has changed here.

Seeland: Ceiling, floor, wall…

Look: Time, air, temperature…

Seeland: The layout and interior…

Look: And this pile of watermelon rind…

Seeland: Remain exactly as they were thirty years ago.

Look: It is still green and smells good.

Pause.

Keung: I can't take it anymore…

Goldy: That's what it means to be professional.

Ken: Sustainable.

Pause.

Seeland: I think…

Ken / 黃金 / 阿強：	我們做地產，有一個信念，就是要幫每個客戶成就他們的人生目標 — 從小單位搬到大單位、從低層搬到高層、從無景搬到有景、從街景搬到山景、從山景搬到海景、從海景搬到無敵海景……在這個過程中，我們跟每一個客戶都心連心，一起努力，朝着最遠大，最高端的目標進發，改變世界，美好人生。

【靜默片刻】

【由現在開始，歐陸和辛西蘭的形態和腔調的「老化」特徵愈趨明顯】

歐陸：　　30 年。

辛西蘭：　30 年如一日。

歐陸：　　這裏好像一切都沒變。

辛西蘭：　天花、地板、牆壁……

歐陸：　　時間、空氣、溫度……

辛西蘭：　一切的格局和佈置……

歐陸：　　還有這一堆西瓜皮……

辛西蘭：　都和 30 年前一樣。

歐陸：　　一樣的翠綠和芬芳。

【靜默片刻】

阿強：　　我快不行啦……

黃金：　　專業就是一個字……

Ken：　　撐。

【靜默片刻】

辛西蘭：　我想……

Look:	Yes?
	Pause.
Seeland:	It's not resolved.
	Pause.
Goldy:	Not resolved?
	Pause.
Keung:	What else do you have to resolve?
	Pause.
Goldy:	Just sign.
	Pause.
Keung:	It's that simple.
	New Seeland moves. She wants to exit. Her gestures become that of an old woman.
Look:	Seeland…
	New Seeland stops.
Ken:	Thirty years.
Goldy:	What are they doing?
Ken:	Our two hour Trial Residency has cost them thirty years of their lives.
Keung:	What?
Ken:	It's like they're using their life credit card. They keep spending incessantly.
Keung:	What the fuck?
Ken:	It's the spirit departing from the flesh.
Goldy:	What the fuck is that?
Ken:	The spirit departs from the flesh and follows its own path.

歐陸： 怎樣？

【靜默片刻】

辛西蘭： 還是未解決。

【靜默片刻】

黃金： 未解決？

【靜默片刻】

阿強： 你們還要解決什麼啊？

【靜默片刻】

黃金： 簽個名就行啦。

【靜默片刻】

阿強： 很簡單的。

【辛西蘭有所行動 — 好像要離去 — 她的形態已然是一個老人了】

歐陸： 「晒冷」……

【辛西蘭停】

Ken： 30 年。

黃金： 他們幹嘛啊？

Ken： 兩個小時的 Trial Residency，他們已經過了 30 年。

阿強； 吓？

Ken： 他們好像在刷卡，將他們的時間不停地刷出去。

阿強： 這麼邪門？

Ken： 這就叫「靈肉異軌」。

黃金： 什麼鳥玩意？

Ken： 靈魂和肉體脫了軌，各行各路。

Keung:	Fuck…
Ken:	Listen.
	The sound of soldiers and horses.
Goldy:	What the fuck is that?
Ken:	Their spirits are taking our flesh into a battlefield.
Keung:	This is fucking crazy!
	Keung opens the door. He exits, but re-enters again immediately.
Keung:	There are thousands of sales agents like Cao Cao flocking in!
Goldy:	This show flat is our city. Our last stand. No one else can fucking enter!
Ken:	Wearing our armour, we fight hundreds of battles. If Liu Lan is not taken we can never return
Keung:	Ken, Goldy and Keung Delta!
	Each of them pulls out a pistol.
Kn/G/Kg:	Many a time I go to my homeland in dreams. Forever my gravestone will face my birthplace.
	They rush out. The sound of shooting can be heard.
	A torrent of time flows with the shots.
	The sound of shooting continues, then gradually change to the sound of shooting arrows.

阿強：　　我操……

Ken：　　你們聽聽。

　　　　　【傳來兵馬之聲】

黃金：　　又是什麼鳥玩意？

Ken：　　他們的靈魂，帶着我們的肉體，走進了一個戰場。

阿強：　　白癡！

　　　　　【阿強打開門 — 出 — 但馬上又衝入】

阿強：　　外面有成千上萬的曹操湧進來啊！

黃金：　　這個單位是我們的城池，最後一個，誰他媽都不能進來！

Ken：　　黃沙百戰穿金甲，不破樓蘭誓不還！

阿強：　　Ken、金、強，三角連線！

　　　　　【三人拔出手槍】

Ken/
黃金 /
阿強：　　活着夢回故土，死後墓向原鄉。

　　　　　【三人向外衝出。槍聲響起】

　　　　　【時間的激流再一次隨着槍聲流竄】

　　　　　【槍聲持續】

　　　　　【槍聲漸變成射箭聲】

第二十二場

Scene 22

Scene 22

Immediately after the previous scene. Time shifts to ancient times.

The scene on the stage turns into a couple of red cliffs.

Ken, Goldy and Keung stand as if they are the sculpture of Liu Bei, Guan Yu and Zhang Fei under the Red Cliff.

Eu Look and New Seeland are getting really old.

Eu Look recites Memories of the Past at Red Cliff by Su Shi.

Look: East flows the mighty river,

           Sweeping away the heroes of times past.

Seeland: This ancient rampart on its western shore

           Is Zhou Yu's Red Cliff of Three Kingdoms' fame;

Look: Here jagged boulders pound the clouds,

           Huge waves tear banks apart,

           And foam piles up a thousand drifts of snow;

Seeland: A scene fair as a painting,

           Countless the brave men, here, in time gone by!

Look: I dream of Marshal Zhou Yu in his day

           With his new bride, the Lord Qiao's younger daughter,

           Dashing and debonair,

Seeland: Silk-capped, with feather fan,

           He laughed and jested

           While the dread enemy fleet was burned to ashes!

第二十二場

【距上場約一秒。時間彷彿回到古代】

【場景彷彿變成幾道「赤壁」】

【Ken、黃金和阿強像一組「劉關張雕塑」，站在「赤壁」之下】

【歐陸與辛西蘭入，兩人已然是垂垂老去】

【歐陸唸誦蘇軾的《赤壁懷古》】

歐陸：　　大江東去，浪淘盡，千古風流人物。

辛西蘭：　故壘西邊，人道是：三國周郎赤壁。

歐陸：　　亂石穿空，驚濤拍岸，捲起千堆雪。

辛西蘭：　江山如畫，一時多少豪傑。

歐陸：　　遙想公瑾當年，小喬初嫁了，雄姿英發。

辛西蘭：　羽扇綸巾，談笑間，檣櫓灰飛煙滅。

Look:	In fancy, through those scenes of old I range,
	My heart overflowing, surely a figure of fun.
	A man grey before his time.
	Pause.
Seeland:	Ah, this life is a dream,
	Let me drink to the moon on the river!
	Pause.
	New Seeland tries to exit.
Look:	Where are you going?
Seeland:	Whether living in a cave or cottage, man used to live on the land. But the buildings nowadays, even the lowest floor, cannot touch the land. Basically, the flats we buy, are all air castles. They are similar to those nests where birds live.
Look:	We've spent so much effort to climb up; it's not easy to come down.
Seeland:	But we are human beings. We are not birds.
	New Seeland exits.
	Pause.
	Eu Look picks up a document and signs.
	Eu Look puts down the document. Exits.
	Ken, Goldy and Keung are left in the show flat. They are still, in the form of the Liu, Guan and Zhang sculpture. They stay quietly in the flat, or, under the Red Cliff.

~End~

歐陸：　　故國神遊，多情應笑我，早生華髮。

　　　　　【靜默片刻】

辛西蘭：　人生如夢，一樽還酹江月。

　　　　　【靜默片刻】

　　　　　【辛西蘭欲下】

歐陸：　　你去哪？

辛西蘭：　以前的人無論住山洞，還是住茅屋，都是住在地下；但是現在的樓，就算最下面那層，其實都碰不到地。基本上，我們買的房子，全都是「空中樓閣」，跟鳥兒住的鳥巢差不多。

歐陸：　　這麼辛苦才上來，下去更不容易啊。

辛西蘭：　但是我們是人吶，我們不是麻雀啊。

　　　　　【辛西蘭下】

　　　　　【靜默片刻】

　　　　　【一份文件從空中掉下】

　　　　　【歐陸下】

　　　　　【單位內，只剩下 Ken、黃金和阿強 － 仍然是一組「劉關張雕塑」，默默地存在於單位內 － 或者，在赤壁之下】

― 劇終 ―

香港藝術節簡介

香港藝術節成立於 1972 年，為國際藝壇重要的表演藝術節之一。每年均帶來近 150 場由本地、亞洲和世界頂尖藝人及團隊精心製作的表演。藝術節的節目色色俱備，既顧及古典傳統口味，亦具備新穎創意和香港難得一見的表演形式，每屆入場觀眾人次高達 12 萬。近年，藝術節與亞洲區內其他藝術節積極合作，孕育新作，與享譽國際的藝術機構聯合委約全新作品，並支持不同領域的藝術家進行跨區跨媒體的合作。此外，香港藝術節「青少年之友」計劃，致力培養年青人對藝術的興趣，過去 19 年間已有近 11 萬名中學生及大學生參與。經過 39 年的發展，今天的藝術節不論在表演藝人數目、演出水平、節目種類各方面，均為本地藝壇之最。

香港藝術節 www.hk.artsfestival.org

香港藝術節的資助來自
The Hong Kong Arts Festival is made possible with the funding support of

香港賽馬會慈善信託基金
The Hong Kong Jockey Club Charities Trust

康樂及文化事務署
Leisure and Cultural Services Department

The Hong Kong Arts Festival

The Hong Kong Arts Festival, first established in 1972, presents close to 150 performances and events by top international, regional, national and local talent during February and March every year. The eclectic mix of classical and contemporary works cater to an audience of about 120,000 including participants of the Festival's Young Friends Scheme. The Festival also commissions, produces and publishes new works independently or in collaboration with international partners. Festival information is available at www.hk.artsfestval.org.

香港藝術節
Hong Kong Arts Festival

督印人 Publisher	何嘉坤 Tisa Ho
主編 Editor	蘇國雲 So Kwok-wan
執行編輯 Executive Editor	鄺潔冰 Cabbie Kwong
助理編輯 Assistant Editor	李宛虹 Lei Yuen Hung
平面設計 排版 Designer	羅美儀 Paula Law
出版 Published by	香港藝術節協會有限公司 Hong Kong Arts Festival Society Limited
印刷 Printer	嘉昱有限公司 Cheer Shine Enterprise Co. Ltd.
版次 Edition	2012 年 2 月初版 1st edition, February 2012
書號 / ISBN	978 988 16056 1 0
定價 / Price	港幣 HK$120
版權垂詢 Copyright Enquiry	香港藝術節協會有限公司 Hong Kong Arts Festival Society Limited

香港灣仔港灣道二號 12 字樓
12/F, 2 Harbour Road, Wan Chai, Hong Kong
電話 Tel : 2824 3555
傳真 Fax : 2824 3798, 2824 3722
網頁 Website : www.hk.artsfestival.org
電郵 Email : afgen@hkaf.org